GEORGE MCGOVERN

GEORGE MCGOVERN

A POLITICAL LIFE, A POLITICAL LEGACY

EDITED BY ROBERT P. WATSON

South Dakota State Historical Society Press

Pierre, South Dakota

Picture credits:
All images are courtesy of Senator George McGovern
Collection, Layne Library, Dakota Wesleyan University,
Mitchell, S.Dak.

Library of Congress Cataloging-in-Publication data
George McGovern : a political life, a political legacy / edited by
Robert P. Watson.
       p. cm.
Includes bibliographical references.
ISBN 0-9715171-6-9
1. McGovern, George S. (George Stanley), 1922–
2. McGovern, George S. (George Stanley), 1922– —Influence.
3. Legislators—United States—Biography. 4. United States.
Congress. Senate—Biography. 5. United States—Politics and
government—1945-1989. 6. United States—Politics and
government—1989- I. Watson, Robert P., 1962–
E840.8.M34G46 2004
973.923′092—dc22

2004013011

ISBN 0-9715171-6-9

Printed in the United States of America

12 11 10 09 08 07 06 05 04

9 8 7 6 5 4 3 2 1

CONTENTS

REEXAMINING THE LIFE AND LEGACY
OF GEORGE MCGOVERN

SENATOR TOM DASCHLE

The Wild Blue, historian Stephen Ambrose's vivid account of the men and boys who flew the B-24s over Germany during the Second World War, gave many people their first glimpse of the *real* George McGovern. Ambrose's retelling of the heroism that won the twenty-two-year-old McGovern the Distinguished Flying Cross surprised people who thought they knew George McGovern.

But it did not surprise the people who know McGovern best: his fellow South Dakotans. We have always known that the caricature created by the Nixon reelection campaign was wrong. We know George McGovern, not only as a war hero, but also as a profoundly decent minister and deeply spiritual man, a thoughtful professor, a fierce champion of family farmers, and one of the most skilled political organizers in South Dakota history. This collection of essays allows others to meet the George McGovern we know. By examining the life and legacy of George McGovern through the eyes of South Dakotans (and a few other experts), editor Robert Watson has given us valuable new insights into a remarkable man.

In 1978, I was elected to the United States House of Representatives. For the next two years, I had the privilege of serving in Congress with George McGovern. Although he was the most senior member of our state's four-person congressional delegation and I was the most junior, he treated me as an equal. He showed me, by his example, that you can express deep convictions without ranting. He also showed me that politics can indeed be a noble profession.

In a speech at Wheaton College in Illinois less than a month before the 1972 election, George McGovern talked about the path that led him to public service. He told his audience: "I felt called into the work of serving others. At first I thought my vocation was in the ministry, and I enrolled in seminary. . . . After a period of deep reflection, I thought I should become a teacher. Yet, even in my teaching at Dakota Wesleyan University, I felt there was something else for me to do—and that is what finally led me into politics." He went on in that speech to say: "We know that the Kingdom of God will not come from a political party's platform. We also know that if someone is hungry, we should give him food; if he is thirsty, we should give him drink; if he is a stranger, we should take him in; if he is naked, we should clothe him; if he is sick, we should care for him; and if he is in prison, we should visit him." That, in simple form, is the story of George McGovern's life and career.

People talk sometimes about "McGovernism." To me, true McGovernism means believing in basic American values—democracy, justice, and the dignity of honest work—and never hesitating to embrace those values, even when they are not popular. McGovernism is having the courage to face the hard issues—like the shame of hunger in America and the reality of the war in Vietnam. It means choosing dialogue over blame, respect over division, hope over fear.

What sets George McGovern apart from many politicians is not simply his compassion and integrity. It is also his uncommon vision. As a senator, he saw connections others did not see—like the connection between piles of surplus grain in America's heartland and hungry children in developing nations. That vision became the Food for Peace program. He also saw things sooner than others did. In 1962, he said, "The most important issue of our time is the establishment of the conditions for world peace." As early as 1970, he warned against over-reliance on our rapidly depleting energy supplies and urged the development of alternative energy sources. In 1984, after he had left the Senate, he implored America's leaders to show strong leadership in the search for peaceful change in the Middle East.

George McGovern's stature as a politician and his decency as a man are reflected in the testimonials his colleagues offered when he left the Senate in 1981. "History will record that George McGovern was a great Senator," predicted Abe Ribicoff. Claiborne Pell, a colleague on the Foreign Relations Committee, said, "He must have been an excellent teacher because he raised the consciousness of his colleagues and demonstrated that there are many ways to solve difficult problems—if only enough intellectual curiosity and imagination are brought to bear." George Mitchell said, "George McGovern was in the forefront of the politics of discussion and debate, of civility and gentlemanliness, of ideas and real issues, of hope and positive action." A man who did not live long enough to see George McGovern leave the Senate but who knew him well and was a close friend said simply, "George McGovern is the most decent man in the U. S. Senate." That man was Robert F. Kennedy. He offered that assessment in South Dakota two months before he died.

One of my favorite descriptions of George McGovern was offered not by a politician but by the columnist and writer Pete Hamill. Back in the 1972 campaign, Hamill wrote: "George McGovern comes at you like one of those big Irish heavyweights in the 1930s—a little slow, but with the chin shut hard against the chest, the jaw breaching out, coming on, daring you to do your best. . . . [H]e might be beaten, but you will know he was there. He will not fold up on you . . . he will surrender no dignity . . . and you will come away speaking about him with respect."

The essays in this book are likely to have the same effect on many readers. Admirers of George McGovern will have their admiration for the man reinforced. And I suspect that even many who disagree with his politics are likely to discover a surprising new respect for the man.

PREFACE

ROBERT P. WATSON

Surveying the American political landscape in the latter half of the twentieth century, it is difficult to find a more compelling figure than George McGovern. Russell Willis, writing in Chapter 8 of this book, eloquently and accurately describes McGovern as a universal man: "decorated warrior, husband and father, professor, grassroots politician, White House bureaucrat, United States congressman and senator, leader of the loyal opposition to the Vietnam War, presidential candidate, writer, social commentator." Indeed, McGovern's contributions to the ongoing American democratic experiment are staggering, in both the sheer breadth of issues he championed and the depth of his commitment and influence. From reforming the Democratic party and the democratic nature of presidential elections, to serving as spokesperson for and moral conscience of the peace movement, to tirelessly advocating for the alleviation of world hunger, George McGovern has led a lifelong crusade for humanity, justice, and equality.

McGovern likes to note that Adlai Stevenson observed that "a wise man does not try to hurry history." With all due respect to the late statesman, I would take issue with Stevenson. With a restless fire in the belly and with revolutionary zeal, the "wise man" has led many a righteous cause. It is true that, more often than not, he has encountered legendary opposition in attempting to bring the rest of society—kicking and screaming—to share his vision. But it is also true that once-radical concepts have often become so readily accepted by us today as to appear commonplace, thanks to such wise men and women. George McGovern has been one such wise and visionary leader. Indeed, few politicians have been labeled as "being ahead of their time" more often than McGovern. And, I am fairly confident, few politicians have turned out to have been on the "right side of history" as often as McGovern.

The book you are about to read is part of a scholarly conference dedicated to the life and political career of George McGovern, which I had the honor of convening. The conference was held in November 2004 on the campus of Dakota Wesleyan University (DWU) in Mitchell, South Dakota, where McGovern both graduated and was a member of the faculty and where plans are underway for the George and Eleanor McGovern Library and Center for Public Service. This McGovern Library and Center is named in honor of the man whose lifelong commitment to public service and learning will be the inspiration for the new facility. Royalties from this book will be donated to the work of the McGovern Library and Center.

My experiences working on the book and associated conference with the faculty, staff, and students of Dakota Wesleyan University led me to appreciate why George McGovern not only chose to enroll as a student and subsequently accept a faculty appointment on campus but why he maintained a long, supportive relationship with the university throughout his life. I recognize and offer a sincere thank you to Robert Duffett, president of DWU, for his enthusiastic support of this project, and to Laurie Langland, university archivist, for her tireless work on behalf of both the book and conference. A number of other individuals with DWU also deserve far more recognition than can be offered in this Preface, especially including Peter Correa, former vice-president for Finance and Administration; Greg Christy, vice-president for Institutional Advancement; Lori Essig, director of University Relations; Rochelle ("Rocky") Von Eye, associate professor of mathematics; and Kevin Kenkel, director of Learning Resources. A special thanks also to Russ Willis, formerly the vice-president for Academic Affairs and dean of DWU and currently the provost and chief academic officer at Champlain College in Vermont, for saying "yes" to my initial proposal for a book and conference and for initiating the popular and important series of McGovern programs at DWU. Thanks also to Donald Watt, the current vice-president and academic dean, who has brought the project to fruition.

Two others, without whom the book would not have been published, deserve acknowledgment. Donald C. Simmons, Jr., executive director of the South Dakota Humanities Council, shared the vision for the book and conference from the outset and was instrumental in bringing all the necessary parties together to make both projects a reality. It was also Simmons who arranged for me to come to South Dakota to speak on a panel with Senator McGovern, which began the process of collaboration among all the aforementioned individuals. I am also deeply indebted to Nancy Tystad Koupal, director of Research and Publishing with the South Dakota State Historical Society, for embracing the proposed book idea and to her able staff, Patti Edman, Jeanne Kilen Ode, Carol Olson, and student intern Laura Ringling, who together put in long hours chasing down facts and making the idea a reality. It is a pleasure to publish this book with the South Dakota State Historical Society Press.

I must admit to having a more enjoyable and rewarding experience than probably anyone else affiliated with this book and conference. Not only did I have the pleasure of working with my capable colleagues who contributed chapters to the book—Gary Aguiar, Ahrar Ahmad, Tom Knock, Valerie O'Regan, Jon Schaff, Donald Simmons, Stephen Stambough, Michael Taylor, Stephen Ward, Russell Willis—and the good people of DWU, but I had the honor of working with two of South Dakota's foremost and finest citizens—two public servants who embody all that politics and elected office should be. There are no finer examples of duty and honor in public life during my lifetime than George McGovern and Tom Daschle. I also had the distinct privilege of serving as the visiting scholar for the inaugural event of the South Dakota Center for the Book, hosted by the South Dakota Humanities Council. I spent a busy but enjoyable week in late summer of 2002 crisscrossing South Dakota speaking to community groups, schools, libraries, and tourists at Mount Rushmore to promote two of my recent books and, more importantly, to promote reading. This travel and promotion proved to be an easy task in South Dakota, as I not only encountered the state's legendary hospitality and scenic landscape, but from one small town to another I came across some of the best-read, most-voracious readers I have ever encountered. It must be said that South Dakota has more bibliophiles per capita than anyplace on earth!

It is a difficult—if not impossible task—to assess the political career and legacy of someone like George McGovern, especially in one brief book. But I hope we have done a worthy job and that you, the reader, find the book informative.

MCGOVERN'S UPBRINGING

IN SOUTH DAKOTA

THE MAKING OF A POLITICAL MIND

DONALD C. SIMMONS, JR.

 *While the dictators built mighty machines of war, Congress debated the advisability of a federal housing plan or an old age pension program. While Hitler spent billions for modern weapons of war, our meager troops had to be satisfied with antiquated left-overs from World War No. 1.[1]*
— George McGovern, age 19

Whether they admire or oppose his politics, many people find it a bit surprising and somewhat disconcerting to think that George McGovern would ever criticize Congress for debating and passing social programs or that he would advocate that General Douglas MacArthur, a military-minded Republican, should be president.[2] We are most comfortable putting people and ideas in categories that can be easily understood and readily identified. Life, however, is much more complicated than we like to think it is, and it is filled with many people and events that do not fit into our preconceived notions of the world or how it should be. Like all of us, George McGovern was once young and impressionable, and he experimented with differing views and opinions of the world in which he lived. McGovern's upbringing in South Dakota greatly influenced his life and political career, and it served as a catalyst for the ever-evolving political views of his youth. It also served as the foundation for the politician he would become.

In the opening chapter of his autobiography, George McGovern described how he felt growing up in the depression era of the 1930s in a middle-class family from South Dakota, watching helplessly as neighbors lost their farms. He described a family friend "sitting on the steps of his back porch, tears streaking his dusty face" because the check from the sale of his pigs at the market did not cover the cost of trucking them to the sale.[3] Even though he was personally protected from the horrors of the Great Depression by his father's meager but steady income as a minister, George saw many of his friends and their families lose everything to choking dust storms and hordes of grasshoppers. He was a child of the depression, and his family listened intently to the "fireside chats" of President Franklin D. Roosevelt, the architect of the New Deal, broadcast by radio into South Dakota. Young McGovern saw what government could do through public works projects and social programs to stabilize the economy and make life better for all Americans.

He also saw President Roosevelt declare war against Japan and Germany in an effort to "make the world safe for democracy." He saw young men go off to war, just as he himself did; and he saw them return as men, changed physically and mentally, just as he was also changed by the experience. For a boy growing up in rural South Dakota, men of action like Roosevelt must have seemed larger than life. Roosevelt defended the poor and helped those who could not help themselves. Outside of McGovern's sheltered home life in Mitchell, South Dakota, it was a world gone mad, but it was the world of George McGovern's youth.

Family and Religion

George S. McGovern was born on 19 July 1922 in the Wesleyan Methodist parsonage in Avon, South Dakota, a small community of about six hundred people located less than fifty miles from Mitchell, the place George would spend much of his childhood and eventually call home. His father, Joseph McGovern, was minister for the tiny Methodist congregation of twenty or so families living in and around Avon before he requested a transfer to Calgary, Alberta, Canada, so that George's mother, Frances McLean McGovern, could care for her sick mother. The family lived in Calgary for two years before returning to South Dakota to make Mitchell their permanent home.

Before becoming a minister and ultimately serving as the spiritual shepherd for the Wesleyan congregation of Mitchell, Joseph McGovern's life had taken many unexpected turns. The oldest child in a family that lost its mother when he was only thirteen, Joseph began working at a young age as a "breaker boy" in a mine, where he followed older miners and picked up missed or dropped pieces of coal. The financial hardships were difficult and, according to some members of the family, they were made worse by their father's drinking. Joseph's father eventually departed from the Catholic teachings he nominally accepted during his youth to embrace the more fundamentalist teachings of John Wesley, leading to the subsequent conversion of Joseph and the other children, as well.[4] Young Joseph, who grew up to be quite athletic, went on to play professional baseball in Des Moines, Iowa, traveling throughout the midwestern United States before using the money he had saved to pay for tuition at the Wesleyan Methodist College in Houghton, New York. His deeply religious convictions would serve as a source of strength for his children. In his autobiography, George McGovern stated that he "never doubted the essential integrity and sincerity of my parents—a priceless parental gift to a child. They gave me a knowledge of the Bible and the Christian faith."[5]

Religion was an overriding factor in George's early life. Every morning in the McGovern household, the day began with the family assembled in the living room for a one- or two-chapter Bible reading followed by prayer. Sunday, of course, was devoted to time at church, and worship services, music rehearsals, and youth meetings filled the rest of the week. Winters and summers were taken up with church-related special activities that were extensions of their faith-dedicated family life. Traveling evangelists frequented their church and Mitchell-area campgrounds, filling the night air with fervent sermons, altar calls, and inspirational music. Young George was not overly impressed with what he later referred to as the "excessive emotionalism of some evangelists." These preachers were nothing like his dignified and restrained father, whose demeanor perhaps explained George's own understated delivery style during his political career. Throughout his life, McGovern credited his religious upbringing and the sincerity of the Wesleyan Methodism embraced by his father for laying the core foundation of his character, especially his concern for the plight of others and his commitment to service above self.[6]

The conservative views of the McGovern parents placed strict limits on the activities of the children. Movies, dancing, and card games, for example, were strictly off limits. Of all the forbidden activities of his youth, movies were the preferred transgression for young George. *Aladdin and His Wonderful Lamp* was the first of many motion pictures he would sneak off to see with friends at the Paramount or the Roxie theater. The forbidden experience of the movies exposed the young McGovern to a world much larger than Mitchell and the state of South Dakota. He financed his trips to the theater, at least once a week, by saving pennies and doing odd jobs like mowing lawns. When he was not working to get money for the movies, he could usually be found at Mitchell's Carnegie Library.

Like many towns around the country at that time, Mitchell enjoyed a well-constructed library with an incredible collection of books, newspapers, journals, and magazines courtesy of the late industrialist Andrew Carnegie. Several times a week, for many hours at a time, McGovern sat at the large oak tables, sometimes completing class assignments, but more often reading stories from the world beyond South Dakota. Books that influenced his early life were Mark Twain's *Tom Sawyer* and *Huckleberry Finn*, Zane Grey's *Riders of the Purple Sage*, and Stuart Chase's *Tyranny of Words*. Of course, he eventually moved on to more serious works of fiction and nonfiction, becoming a compulsive reader and frequently engaging friends in discussions and debates about issues raised by his favorite authors.

While dancing was forbidden in the McGovern household, music was not. The family enjoyed playing records on the phonograph and listening to WNAX, a popular radio station in Yankton. Church services were filled with hymns and the musical groups that often accompanied the evangelists who came to town. Glee club and chorus concerts were regular events on the family calendar. It was the era of Glenn Miller, Benny Goodman, and Tommy Dorsey, and the McGovern children enjoyed the music of the day.[7]

Education and Debate

Young George McGovern did not, however, arrive in Mitchell the well-spoken, reasoned, and confident debater he would later become as a national politician. As a child, he was quite shy and reserved, so bashful, in fact, that his first-grade teacher incorrectly assumed his reluctance to speak meant he was not a proficient reader and passed him to second grade "on condition." He was so shy that on one occasion he urinated on himself while waiting for the classroom bell rather than raise his hand and ask to be excused. It would be his second-grade teacher, pressuring young George to read aloud in class and keeping him after school to read passages aloud, who forced him to shed his shy disposition. He credits much of his later success to her determination and words of assurance. McGovern also recalls the assistance of two high-school teachers, Rose Hopfner and Bob Pearson, who not only helped to prepare him for the academic challenges that lay ahead, but also taught him the skills needed by a successful politician.[8]

Hopfner, his sophomore English-composition teacher, praised the future senator for his ability to use the written and spoken word to express himself. She encouraged him to speak with Pearson, the history teacher and debate coach, about joining the high-school debate team. According to McGovern, Pearson did more to give him confidence and "draw out his latent powers of expression" than anyone else.[9] Through competitive debate, young McGovern was transformed. The exercise forced him to organize his thoughts, to find evidence to support his point of view, and to look at both sides of complex issues. Debate became his obsession. He spent nights and weekends studying and discussing issues with his debate partner, Eddie Mizel.[10] Using three-by-five note cards, the partners maintained a library of data and statistics available at a moment's notice if needed for competition. They relished the idea of trying to sway individuals to consider alternative points of view when important matters of the day were concerned. They won their first debate competition and first trophies as sophomores, and by their senior year in high school, they were nearly unstoppable. College scholarships were their ultimate reward for traveling to many competitions in Bob Pearson's car.

While McGovern was typically a serious competitor, who stayed focused on the competition, he did get somewhat distracted when facing the squad from Woonsocket, a tiny community of about eight hundred located about thirty miles northwest of Mitch-

ell. Ila and Eleanor Stegeberg, eye-catching young twins, captured George's attention. On one occasion, Ila and Eleanor's team
handed McGovern and Mizel their only defeat. The Stegebergs
were not easily forgotten, but McGovern was reticent around
women and saw no future in trying to court girls who lived so far
away.[11]

When he graduated from high school in the spring of 1940,
George McGovern was one of the region's best young orators. He
not only graduated third in his class of 140, he was also selected
"The Most Representative Senior Boy."[12] His education and extracurricular activities had prepared him well for the rigors and challenges of academe as he began his studies at Dakota Wesleyan University (DWU) that fall. Unlike most students of the day, he was
also relatively well traveled, having taken a number of family vaca-
tions throughout the Midwest and even to Canada, and was quite
knowledgeable about the topics of the day.

DWU and Eleanor

When George McGovern began his college career in the fall
of 1940, the days of the Great Depression were all but a distant memory, but an equally ominous threat was on the hori-
zon. The nationalistic fervor promoted by ideologues like Adolph
Hitler and Benito Mussolini was sweeping across Europe and
Asia, fueled by the frustrations of populations suffering some of
the more dire economic conditions of the twentieth century. To
McGovern and his fellow classmates at Dakota Wesleyan University, the political uprisings and fighting abroad must have seemed
remote early in the year, but by November 1940, members of the
South Dakota National Guard's 147th Field Artillery Regiment
were being called to active duty status. Many Dakota Wesleyan students had joined the guard as a way of earning additional money
for college expenses. All around him, these classmates were now
preparing for war abroad.[13]

Nevertheless, McGovern's first years of college were typical, except that he lived and ate at home in order to save money. He excelled academically his first semester as a freshman, as might be
expected, and by the following spring had become a member of
the national forensics honor fraternity, Pi Kappa Delta. To supple-

ment his scholarship, he worked a variety of odd jobs, including candling eggs and as a college recruiter, to pay for miscellaneous expenses.[14] Social activities also began to consume more of his time.

The Stegeberg twins had also decided to attend Dakota Wesleyan, Eleanor as a business major and Ila as a nursing student. Initially, it looked as though the twins would not be able to attend college because their father had only saved two hundred dollars for that purpose, but the promise of secretarial jobs at DWU for twenty-five cents an hour made it possible for them to enroll in the fall of 1940. The Mitchell Roller Rink served as the catalyst for a reunion of the former adversaries of South Dakota high-school debate and the beginning of a lifetime together for George and Eleanor. Instead of shy George taking the initiative, it was Ila who took the lady's-choice skate as an opportunity to approach him. When the skate was over, George discovered that Ila was already dating a friend of his but Eleanor was available. It was the beginning of what would eventually become a lengthy courtship for the two.

Eleanor and George spent a great deal of time together over the next two years, going to movies and drinking sodas at popular spots around Mitchell. They often attended thrice-weekly chapel together, and evening walks holding hands were common. The university did not allow dancing at social gatherings so students would "stroll" around the gymnasium while music played in the background. Eleanor eventually went home with George to meet his parents, minus her usual coating of lipstick, of course, in order to meet with their favor.[15]

Eleanor's father, Earl Stegeberg, a widower who had raised the girls with the help of their grandfather, immediately liked the intelligent young man who showed up late one evening to pick up his daughter, only to discover that she had given up on her suitor and left with another couple. Earl loved discussing politics, and what began as polite conversation that evening resulted in a discussion of politics and the nature of women. Eleanor, who understood her suitor, later noted that George probably had a better time with her father than he would have had at the dance.[16]

By fall of 1941, the young couple began to make plans for a

future together after college graduation. McGovern had decided to become a history teacher, something he had considered almost from the day he met Bob Pearson, the history teacher and debate coach who inspired him. Eleanor planned to take a job as a legal secretary in Mitchell, working for former United States senator Herbert Hitchcock and attorney Fred Nichol. For the young couple in love, almost oblivious to the rapidly changing world around them, life was good. They did things most college sophomores do. George competed in the fall Freshman/Sophomore Competition, where his tug-o'-war team won first prize. He became president of the sophomore class and the P.K.s (preachers' kids), secretary-treasurer of the Young Men's Christian Association, and toast-master of the Blue and White Day Banquet. The storm of war in Europe was not yet a reality to them, only something they heard about in the news or discussed at their respective family dinner tables. They talked of politics and the coming war with their college friends, but only in the way all college students discuss things of which they have no firsthand knowledge or experience.[17]

Then, Sunday, 7 December 1941, as George sat at home listening to a radio broadcast of the New York Philharmonic for an assignment for Professor Robert Brown's course in music appreciation, John Daly's voice interrupted with the shocking news that the Japanese had bombed the American naval base at Pearl Harbor. Suddenly, the war that had seemed so distant and unreal had changed their lives forever. George and Eleanor had to reevaluate everything; their plans for marriage would be put on hold, perhaps for several years. George tried to convince Eleanor that there was no need to rush into marriage if he were to be shipped somewhere on the other side of the world because he might not return.[18] He even advised other women that they should prepare for the possibility of life after the war without a husband, or even the potential for a husband. In a blunt article published in the college newspaper, he said, "plan for marriage girls, but if it doesn't come, and it cannot come to some of you, take it on the chin and demonstrate to society that the single woman can perform as noble a service as the wife or mother."[19] He was well aware that America would suffer many casualties during the conflict.

McGovern suddenly became obsessed with the war in both

Europe and the Pacific, as well as with support of the American war effort. He wrote numerous articles criticizing those he believed were being too lighthearted about the war. On one occasion, he publicly criticized several DWU students for dancing at the College Inn to the song "Let's Remember Pearl Harbor." In his own words at the time, he acknowledged his extremism when he said, "Now, perhaps my reaction to this dastardly Japanese attack may appear far-fetched—perhaps even cruel and unreasoning," but that did not stop McGovern from criticizing those who did not conduct themselves in the most appropriate manner given the circumstances.[20] He also became obsessed with General Douglas MacArthur, stating on one occasion, "I think MacArthur will be elected to the presidency because he has proven himself to be a real red-blooded American leader."[21] McGovern was critical of anyone who questioned the war effort or anything American, especially MacArthur.

There was no question in McGovern's mind that eventually the United States would prevail in the war. The totalitarian powers were bent on destroying freedom in the world, and he wanted to be part of the war effort. Even so, he hoped that he would have enough time to finish his coursework at DWU before the call to service came. When President Roosevelt declared war soon after the bombing by Japan, McGovern was nineteen and just finishing his first semester as a sophomore. He was the newly elected class president, serving the first of three terms he would earn during his tenure at DWU. His extracurricular activities, however, did not distract him from his studies. He excelled in the classroom, where a number of the faculty were beginning to notice him. Graduate school was becoming a real possibility for the talented and articulate young man.[22]

For the 1941–1942 school year, DWU hired a recent University of Denver graduate, Raymond DeBoer, as the new speech instructor and debate coach. The University of Denver was well respected in the region and nationally for its successful forensics teams. DeBoer's influence on McGovern and the rest of the DWU team was almost immediate. The year proved to be one of the most successful in the team's history. Instead of finishing eighth or worse at regional competitions, as he had done the previous year, McGovern finished first in numerous local and regional meets as the team dominated competitions. McGovern won the 1942 South Dakota Peace Oratory Contest for his speech titled "My Brother's Keeper," which was later recognized by the National Council of Churches as one of the twelve best in the United States that year. After a less-than-stellar showing as a freshman debater, there may have been concern that McGovern would not be competitive at the collegiate level, but now under the tutelage of his new coach and with his new partner Matt Smith, McGovern put to rest any concerns his coach or anyone else may have had about his oratory skills.[23]

War and Marriage

February of 1943 would prove to be the best and the worst of times for McGovern and his new fiancée. He and Eleanor were returning home to Mitchell after a successful competition in Moorhead, Minnesota. George had just been named "best debater" in a five-state tournament, and Matt Smith had come in second. When the bus pulled into Mitchell, Matt's father was there to meet them, extending one hand "in congratulation and the other hand clutching the induction notice that had arrived earlier that day for George."[24] The induction notice was a severe blow for McGovern, who preferred to plan things well in advance. Soon after the bombing of Pearl Harbor, he had gone with a group of ten friends to the recruiting station in Omaha in anticipation of future service. He spoke with representatives of both the navy and army and had finally decided, along with the rest of his friends, to join the army because it was said to be handing out free lunch passes. It had never occurred to McGovern that he might not have time to finish his junior year, but if he had to go, he wanted to fight only one way, and that was in the air. He and all ten of his friends who went on that trip to Omaha joined the United States Army Air Forces.[25]

Ironically, as a favor to his friend Norman Ray, who loved flying, McGovern had agreed to sign up for a Civil Aeronautics Administration flight-instruction course offered by the college and the federal government at the Mitchell airport. DWU had only been offering the course for two years but had already trained forty-five pilots, including several women. When the war began, the federal government refused to allow women to participate in the program in favor of men who could be sent on for further combat train-ing, if needed. George easily passed the required physical exami-nation and was admitted to the program. Nine other students from around the region were also admitted to the class, although one of them, John Simmons, left for the army air forces after completion of ground school.

Like most of his classmates, McGovern enjoyed the ground-school classes, which consisted of seventy-two hours of instruc-tion on things like air regulations, aircraft repair, meteorology, and navigation, but when he got up in the air, he initially hated it. Just the thought of flying, he told Eleanor, was frightening. He was not alone in his fear, and several of the students vomited during their first flights, according to instructor C. A. Ramynke. McGov-ern survived the lessons, soloed, and flew the required thirty-five-plus hours in the air, working quickly to complete his hours much sooner than most of his fellow classmates. His class of nine fin-ished with the highest scores of any class in the state that year on their ground-school exams.[26] In his autobiography, McGovern stated that as a student pilot he "was nervous, but I also felt a sense of exhilaration."[27]

McGovern boarded the train in February 1943 and began his life as a member of the United States armed forces. The horror of war would soon become real for the son of a preacher from a small town in South Dakota. McGovern flew thirty-five bomb-ing missions over Europe. His plane was hit numerous times, but he managed to keep it in the air and land his crew safely after every bombing mission. McGovern returned to Mitchell after his discharge from the service in the summer of 1945. Eleanor met him in Minneapolis, and they rode the train back to South Dakota together.[28]

During the war, life had changed for George McGovern, just as it had changed for South Dakota and the rest of the world. He and Eleanor had been married on 31 October 1943 while he was on a three-day leave from flight training at Muskogee, Oklahoma. McGovern's father had died while he was away, leaving him with a sense of responsibility for his mother's well-being, and his first child, Ann, was born during his absence. He now had all the re-sponsibilities of a family. Thanks to the GI Bill, he could afford to finish his education, and he enrolled in school immediately upon his return. It was a difficult time for him as he suffered from what today would be known as post-traumatic stress syndrome. Nightmares and visions of combat-related events plagued him for a considerable length of time.[29]

McGovern looked for the answers to his questions about life in books as he resumed his studies at DWU. Professor Don McAninch, a philosophy instructor, became his mentor, encouraging McGovern to ponder value systems and the meaning of life. In his autobiography, McGovern said that McAninch's course, assigned readings, and the subsequent discussions had "a profound effect on my own intellectual and spiritual development."[30] During that time, McGovern decided to forego Wesleyan Methodism for the less fundamentalist mainstream Methodist church, which was more in line with his own views. He also decided to become a minister.[31]

Like most veterans who returned from fighting World War II, McGovern initially felt as though he had fought the war to end all wars, the last great war, but as the Cold War became a reality, he began to express his concerns about war and his hope for peace. In his postwar, award-winning entry in the state Peace Oratory Contest, titled "Cave to Cave," one begins to see a hint of the new-thinking McGovern. He began the speech with a commentary on the abuses of American power. He expressed concern that for Americans "maximum financial return" was a "greater concern than human welfare." He was no longer enamored with military leaders like Douglas MacArthur, who did run for president as a Republican candidate in 1952. Instead, McGovern preferred to quote Ghandi and call for "international cooperation," a far cry from the words of the war hawk who had departed for Europe only a few years prior.[32]

Even before graduating from DWU, McGovern had been accepted to Garrett Theological Seminary of Illinois and appointed student minister at Diamond Lake, a community about thirty miles from Evanston, where the seminary was located. Diamond Lake was well suited for the young minister. The congregation was small (rarely more than twenty persons attended services), leaving plenty of time for reading and study. The parsonage was provided

George and Eleanor McGovern, with daughters Susan and Ann, stand outside the Diamond Lake Community Church, where George served as a student minister in 1946–1947.

rent free, allowing the family to spend their meager earnings on other things. The situation initially seemed ideal to George. He quickly discovered, however, that writing thoughtful and inspirational sermons was only a small part of a minister's job; counseling people and visiting the sick consumed much more of his time, and it was something he did not enjoy. He became disillusioned and suffered from depression.[33]

McGovern's Political Education

By late 1947, McGovern had accepted the fact that a minister's life was not his future, and he enrolled in the graduate history program at Northwestern University. A teaching fellowship and a Hearst Fellowship provided enough funding to allow him to pursue his course of study. While at Northwestern, McGovern became even more interested in the study of the social and political struggles of the underclass. The selected topic of his dissertation was the Colorado Coal Strike of 1913–1914 and the Ludlow Massacre. The miners' strike had turned deadly when miners were shot and women and children burned to death by the hired thugs and Colorado militia who were brought in to break the strike. It was a surprising shift in interests for a man who had previously warned others to be wary of labor organizations. Philosophically and politically, McGovern was moving to the left.[34]

During the 1948 elections, McGovern supported a variety of anti-Cold War candidates and causes. He adamantly supported Progressive party candidate Henry Wallace for president, returning to Mitchell to speak on behalf of his candidacy. Wallace had served as FDR's secretary of agriculture and later his vice-president. McGovern denounced those who called Wallace a crackpot and a communist, but no broad base of support for Wallace's candidacy ever developed at the national level. As an Illinois delegate to the national convention of the Progressive party that year, McGovern discovered that many supporters were more liberal and fanatical than he had thought, some even embracing communist positions. McGovern's biographer, Robert Sam Anson, records that McGovern returned from the convention disillusioned with the Wallace campaign and did not vote that year.[35] It was an episode in his political life that he has been at times reluctant to discuss, as was his earlier support of conservative causes such as the potential presidential bid of General MacArthur. McGovern had experimented politically with both the left and the right and, by the end of his studies at Northwestern University, began to formulate his own political philosophy and ideology, one that would remain essentially unchanged throughout his long and distinguished political career.

While completing the writing of his doctoral dissertation at Northwestern, McGovern returned to DWU in 1950 to teach history and serve as the debate team coach. Now at home in Mitchell, McGovern soon became a popular professor and well-respected family man in the community. Unlike other members of the faculty who did not have roots in South Dakota, McGovern could relate to the students who attended DWU. He knew how to inspire them. Dakota Wesleyan's forensics team excelled with McGovern as coach, often going multiple rounds without a loss and winning first place in oratory. By the spring of 1954, the year the first freshman class he coached at DWU became seniors, Dakota Wesleyan's debate team dominated the Sioux Province Tournament. One of his students finished first in the women's peace oratory division that same year. McGovern enjoyed coaching debate so much that even after he no longer taught at the college he continued to coach the DWU team. The conservative college administration permitted this arrangement in spite of the fact that McGovern was now a political activist for the Democratic party of South Dakota.

Even though McGovern's political leanings were a bit more liberal than those of most South Dakotans, Mitchell's community leaders accepted the young professor and even encouraged his political activities. While at least one member of the DWU faculty was fired by the conservative university board for his outspoken liberal views during the era of McCarthyism and the hunt for Communists by the House Un-American Activities Committee, McGovern's activities went virtually unchecked. He had almost complete freedom to select the courses he taught, and he wrote and published letters to the editor of the Mitchell newspaper, gave speeches on behalf of the Democratic party, and spoke for the party on the radio. He was even allowed to take students to party functions while on the way to debate competitions. On one occasion, while on the way to the Rocky Mountain Speech Tournament, McGovern and three of his students made a planned detour to Philip to attend the Democratic party's Jefferson-Jackson Day Dinner, where McGovern addressed the crowd.[36]

By 1952, the McGovern family, with a total of four children, struggled on his meager annual salary of $4,600. Like many first-time faculty, McGovern sought employment at a more prestigious and better-paying university as completion of his Ph.D. neared. He applied to teach at several schools, including the University of Iowa and the University of Denver, but jobs were scarce with so many highly educated veterans seeking employment. In 1953, he resigned his full-time faculty position at DWU to work as an organizer for the South Dakota Democratic Party.[37]

The formative years of McGovern's youth in South Dakota, combined with his early adulthood spent at DWU and in Illinois, helped to shape the man he was to become: articulate, analytical, knowledgeable, and well spoken. It had not been a foregone conclusion that the minister's son from Mitchell would become a social activist and critic of American intervention abroad, but circumstances were such that, while he experimented with many positions within the political spectrum, McGovern ultimately declared himself a Democrat. The political mind of George McGovern had evolved and matured during those formative years, laying the foundation for a politician with tremendous potential. McGovern was positioned to embark on one of the most successful political careers in the history of South Dakota.

NOTES

1. George McGovern, "As I See It," *Phreno Cosmian*, 27 Jan. 1942. McGovern contributed regularly to this column in the *Phreno Cosmian*, which was the student newspaper at Dakota Wesleyan University, Mitchell, South Dakota.

2. Ibid., 24 Mar. 1942.

3. McGovern, *Grassroots: The Autobiography of George McGovern* (New York: Random House, 1977), p. 10.

4. Robert Sam Anson, *McGovern: A Biography* (New York: Holt, Rinehart & Winston, 1972), pp. 16–17; McGovern, *Grassroots*, pp. 3–4.

5. McGovern, *Grassroots*, p. 4.

6. Ibid., p. 5. *See also* Anson, *McGovern*, pp. 20–21.

7. McGovern, *Grassroots*, pp. 13–14. For a delightful account of another boyhood spent in Mitchell in this era, *see* G. D. ("Don") Lillibridge's "Small-Town Boys: Growing Up in Mitchell in the 1920s and 1930s," *South Dakota History* 25 (Spring 1995): 1–36.

8. McGovern, *Grassroots*, pp. 11–12.

9. Ibid., p. 12. *See also* Eleanor McGovern with Mary Finch Hoyt, *Uphill: A Personal Story* (Boston: Houghton Mifflin Co., 1974), pp. 52–53.

10. For more on Mizel, *see* Lillibridge, "Small-Town Boys," pp. 1, 11–14.

11. Anson, *McGovern*, pp. 30–32.

12. McGovern, *Grassroots*, p. 16.

13. Ibid., p. 19; Robert F. Karolevitz, "Life on the Home Front: South Dakota in World War II," *South Dakota History* 19 (Fall 1989): 394, 414; Robert G. Webb, "The Pacific Odyssey of Capt. William H. Daly and the 147th Field Artillery Regiment, 1941–1946," *South Dakota History* 23 (Summer 1993): 102.

14. *Phreno Cosmian*, 18 Dec. 1940, 3 June 1941; Anson, *McGovern*, p. 33.

15. Eleanor McGovern and Hoyt, *Uphill*, pp. 56–57; Anson, *McGovern*, p. 33.

16. McGovern, *Grassroots*, p. 22.

17. Ibid., pp. 17, 20–21; *Phreno Cosmian*, 10 Mar. 1942; Anson, *McGovern*, p. 34.

18. McGovern, *Grassroots*, p. 19; Anson, *McGovern*, p. 34.

19. McGovern, "As I See It," *Phreno Cosmian*, 10 Mar. 1942.

20. McGovern, "A Student Views U. S. Entrance in World War No. 2," ibid., 16 Dec. 1941.

21. McGovern, "As I See It," ibid., 24 Mar. 1942.

22. Anson, *McGovern*, p. 35.

23. "Forensics," *Tumbleweed* (1942): 70–71; Anson, *McGovern*, pp. 34–35. The *Tumbleweed* is the DWU student yearbook.

24. Anson, *McGovern*, p. 35.

25. McGovern, *Grassroots*, p. 20; Anson, *McGovern*, pp. 34–35. The United States Army Air Forces were established in June 1941, comprising the former Army Air Corps and the Air Force Combat Command. Walter J. Boyne, *Beyond the Wild Blue: A History of the United States Air Force, 1947–1997* (New York: St. Martin's Press, 1997), p. 365.

26. *Phreno Cosmian*, 7 Oct., 4 Nov., 9 Dec. 1941; Anson, *McGovern*, pp. 35–36.

27. McGovern, *Grassroots*, p. 19.

28. Ibid., pp. 22–30. The story of McGovern's war experiences is also told in Stephen E. Ambrose, *The Wild Blue: The Men and Boys Who Flew the B-24s over Germany* (New York: Simon & Schuster, 2001).

29. Anson, *McGovern*, pp. 37, 49–50.

30. McGovern, *Grassroots*, p. 32.

31. Anson, *McGovern*, pp. 50–51.

32. Quoted ibid., pp. 51–52.

33. Ibid., pp. 53–54.

34. McGovern, *Grassroots*, pp. 38–39, 47–48; Anson, *McGovern*, pp. 56–57. *See also* McGovern and Leonard F. Guttridge, *The Great Coalfield War* (Boston: Houghton Mifflin Co., 1972).

35. Anson, *McGovern*, pp. 58–61.

36. "Forensics," *Tumbleweed* (1955): 45; Anson, *McGovern*, pp. 63–65; McGovern, *Grassroots*, pp. 50–51.

37. Anson, *McGovern*, pp. 65–66.

CHAPTER TWO

THE VIOLENCE OF WAR

AND THE MARK OF LEADERSHIP

THE SIGNIFICANCE OF MCGOVERN'S AIR

FORCE SERVICE DURING WORLD WAR II

MICHAEL J. C. TAYLOR

 War is the most horrific spectacle of man's inhumanity towards his fellow man. By sheer force, the will of one nation is imposed upon another for reasons that range from jingoistic greed to the overpowering of evil in what President John F. Kennedy termed "the vindication of right."[1] Public threats of military force are made between conflicting countries; weapons are mass-produced, stockpiled, and issued; and nations mobilize the strongest among them to perpetrate violence upon an enemy in the name of, among other justifications, God and country. It is a time when intelligence and reason give way to stark belligerence and consuming force—when might truly does make right. In the end, when the bloodshed and destruction have become too much for its citizens, one side capitulates to the will of the other, and peace is determined based upon the victor's terms.

Still, there are those who have witnessed such conflagration yet refused to view such events within the glow of nationalistic fervor; indeed, war has had the opposite influence on the judgments and deeds of select leaders. For example, historian Margaret Leech says of the twenty-fifth president's service in the Union army during the Civil War: "[William] McKinley left the army with an abiding hatred of war, and a strong belief that arbitration was a civilized principle, which should prevail in the settlement of all disputes."[2] According to Woodrow Wilson biographer August Heckscher, the president's experiences as a small child in Virginia during the Civil War influenced him as president, when, at the cusp of the First World War five decades later, Wilson chose not to wage war for its own sake but to struggle for lasting peace through the creation of "unity and stability in the world around him."[3] Perhaps Brigadier General and later President of the United States Franklin Pierce responded to war with the most candor. "There can be no such thing," he wrote, "as a profound sense of justice, the sacredness of individual rights and the value of human life connected with human butchery."[4]

World War II was an excellent example of the costs of war. In loss of life, the numbers of military personnel varied between 15 and 20 million, with no firm estimates on the enormous numbers of civilian dead. Thousands of people are still unaccounted for; their remains concealed from history and memory. Economically, the cost of war was estimated, in 1945 terms, at over $1 trillion, with United States expenditures of over $330 billion and Adolph Hitler's Third Reich at over $230 billion. The conflict left entire countries incapable of sustaining existence for those left in its wake, and massive relief efforts were undertaken—such as the Marshall Plan launched by the Truman Administration in the late 1940s—in order to keep governments from falling victim once again to radicalism and their citizens from starving to death. In the end, the United States and the Union of Soviet Socialist Republics emerged as the foremost superpowers with a profound distrust of one another that provided the foundation for a cold war lasting nearly five decades. But the devastation of this war also had at least one positive development—the creation of the United Nations, the realization of Woodrow Wilson's dream of a world organization dedicated to the cause of peace, where nations could settle their differences amicably without resorting to death and mass destruction.

The war itself was caused by the breakdown of the worldwide economy at the end of the 1920s, which led to the invasion of China by Japan, of Ethiopia by Italy, and of both Central and Eastern Europe by Nazi Germany. In an effort to gain consistent energy supplies for its industrial economy, Japan conquered Manchuria in 1931. In violation of the Treaty of Versailles, the agreement that had ended the previous world conflict, Chancellor Adolph Hitler began his rearming of Germany. Amidst the arena of the Spanish Civil War in the mid-1930s, innovative German weapons were tested and perfected. From these menacing origins, augmented by the subjugation of sovereign nations throughout Europe, Africa, and Asia, the next clash of rival forces arose.[5]

Most Americans, however, were not paying attention to world affairs. They were fighting to survive dire economic conditions—especially in farming communities in such states as South Dakota, where residents were suffering through the Dust Bowl. For many, the first hint of a second world war came on 7 December 1941, the day the Japanese successfully implemented a surprise attack on the United States naval base at Pearl Harbor, Hawaii. When the announcements were made to an unsuspecting public, Americans were not only stunned at the loss of life but by the fact that a small country could perpetrate such a deed on a big, nonhostile country. It was while sitting in his living room listening to a classical music program on the family radio—a requirement for a music appreciation course at Dakota Wesleyan University—that college student George Stanley McGovern heard of the hostilities. As was the rest of the nation, the McGovern family of Mitchell, South Dakota, was both numbed and angered. "It did not surprise me," McGovern wrote later of the event, "to hear President [Franklin] Roosevelt call within a matter of hours for a declaration of war. What surprised me was the awesome skill and power demonstrated by the Japanese in a succession of air and naval victories which followed."[6] Unbeknownst to the college sophomore, his odyssey as a war pilot had just begun.

Preparations for War

A few months prior to FDR's call to arms, George McGovern had already taken his initial steps toward his destiny, enrolling in flying lessons at the behest of his close friend Norman Ray. The Roosevelt Administration had implemented a civilian pilot training program, which required a total of ten students per session. Ray had wanted to fly all his life, and this program offered the perfect opportunity. He hustled tenaciously until he found the required number of enrollees. Overcoming his apprehension, McGovern joined. "But if I had known what was ahead," he said later, "I never would have enrolled." Controlling his fear and nausea, the nineteen-year-old McGovern completed his training in the fall of 1941. It was also during these courses that the college sophomore viewed the B-24 bomber for the first time as it sat on an auxiliary runway at Mitchell Airport.[7]

After the declarations of war against the Axis powers, and after the country began to mobilize for armed confrontation, ten Dakota Wesleyan University students in two separate automobiles journeyed to Omaha, Nebraska, in the spring of 1942 and enlisted in the armed forces. For these young, educated men, the decision was clear. "We were confronted with totalitarian powers bent on the destruction of freedom," McGovern said, "and that was all I needed to know."[8] Due to his earlier pilot training, McGovern chose to serve in the United States Army Air Forces. The students were not inducted at that time, but all signed an agreement that they would report when called into active duty—an agreement that, for the time being, deferred them from the draft. The notice to report to duty came in February of the following year. As members of the DWU debate team, McGovern and his partner Matt Smith had just emerged as the two most-gifted speakers at the Red River Valley Tournament—a competition that hosted over one hundred of the best teams from the region. Upon their return, McGovern was handed his induction notice. Along with student body president Walter Kriman, he was to report to Jefferson Barracks, Missouri, within seventy-two hours.[9]

The young pilot received his initial air-force flight training at Muskogee, Oklahoma. During a three-day leave, McGovern hurriedly traveled home and married his college sweetheart, Eleanor Stegeberg, on the afternoon of Halloween 1943. The groom's father performed the ceremony. "Our honeymoon consisted of a night at my home in Mitchell," McGovern later recalled, "and then a long train ride to Muskogee in a dirty coach equipped with hard straight-backed seats." The young pilot's training took him next to Coffeeville, Kansas, where he was stationed for ten weeks, and then on to advanced training school at Pampa, Texas. During their extended stay in the Lone Star State, Eleanor McGovern broke the news to her husband that they were going to be parents. Though George was apprehensive about impending parenthood, he came to understand the circumstances: "I felt she [Eleanor] was desperate to be pregnant before I went into combat because, as she acknowledged years later, she would have a child from our marriage

Eleanor McGovern pins silver wings on newly commissioned Second Lieutenant George McGovern at his graduation ceremony in Pampa, Texas, in April 1944.

even if I failed to survive the war."[10] Indeed, countless children came into the world as the living legacies of fathers who did not return from war.

From advanced flight training at Pampa, the McGoverns traveled to Liberal, Kansas, where he was to train in flying the B-24. The primary instructor at the base was none other than Lieutenant Norman Ray, the man who had first coaxed McGovern into taking flying lessons. Following his initial flights on the aircraft, the young pilot emerged apprehensive about the plane known as the Liberator: "The B-24 was a difficult plane to fly. It had a wingspan of 110 feet, and this long, narrow Davis wing seemed to defy aerodynamics. The plane—at that time the biggest in the Air Force—did not have the lift of the B-17 Flying Fortress; it ate up every foot of an average runway before lifting off. Nor did it offer the handling ease of the B-17; its controls were stiff and it exhausted its pilots in formation flying."[11] Following a rigorous training regimen, Second Lieutenant McGovern was designated as a pilot and transferred to Lincoln, Nebraska, where he met his comrades-in-arms, the airmen who would serve their tour of duty under his command. Between June and September 1944, McGovern became acquainted with his crew at Mountain Home, Idaho, as they learned to work as a team. In September, they were assigned to the 741st Squadron of the Fifteenth Air Force and transferred to the European theater, shipping out of Topeka, Kansas.[12]

War Pilot

When McGovern and his crew were assigned to the Fifteenth Air Force, they became part of a newly created unit that had already earned the kudos of both the military and the public-at-large. Established in November 1943 under the command of Lieutenant General Carl A. Spaatz, the Fifteenth had performed successful raids on a myriad of vital military targets in Germany and the occupied countries. The Fifteenth's fliers had delivered devastating blows to Hitler's war capabilities, destroying a Messerschmitt plant at Wiener-Neustadt in Austria, a ball-bearing plant in Genoa, Italy, and a U-boat port in Toulon, France. Other notable targets included the railway yards and ports in Athens, Greece, in January 1944, cutting off Germany's foremost supply line to and from Eastern Europe. Simultaneous offensives on the naval bases at Toulon and railway yard at Florence in March 1944 crippled Germany's ability to hold territory around the Mediterranean. An aircraft manufacturing plant in Belgrade, Yugoslavia, was thoroughly destroyed in April 1944. Throughout the following months, the fliers of the Fifteenth Air Force continued their successful raids, the bulk of which were conducted from their base near Cerignola, Italy.[13]

It was there that the crew of the plane that would later come to be known as the *Dakota Queen* reported for duty. Lieutenant McGovern first served as copilot in a series of five air-raid missions — on marshaling yards in Linz, Austria, on 11 November 1944; on marshaling yards in Györ, Hungary, on 17 November; on a German airfield near Vicenza, Italy, on the eighteenth; a German oil refinery near Vienna, Austria, on the following day; and another on war materials factories in Zlin, Czechoslovakia, the day after that. These missions were a baptism of fire that was meant to acquaint junior officers with the realities of aerial combat. They also counted toward the magic number of thirty-five that guaranteed both an honorable discharge from the war and a cherished ticket home. Though each of the Liberator fighter planes had been equipped with APS-15 radar (nicknamed "Mickey" by the pilots), which had dramatically increased the accuracy of aerial raids during its initial use in spring 1944, on these first missions the targets were sighted visually as a means of instruction.[14] The men involved viewed these missions as little more than "milk runs," but they were reported in the press as a plan of strategic bombings that "virtually guarantees that Adolph Hitler's Reich will wilt."[15]

On 6 December 1944, Lieutenant McGovern undertook his first mission as a commander, and with it came the lessons that mature a man into a leader. Not only did the young officer learn to make crucial decisions at a moment's notice, but he also witnessed the dreadful consequence of crossing the boundary of human endurance. McGovern was nervous because the marshaling yards at Graz, Austria, were the assigned target and were heavily protected by German antiaircraft battalions. "There is no tolerance of error in handling any airplane — but especially a four-engine bomber in combat," he noted.[16] It was critical that under such duress everybody function well, both as individuals and as a team, for their survival depended upon it. Crew and commander were concerned about the excessive weight of the aircraft. For a B-24 (carrying bombs, gasoline, oxygen tanks, and machine-gun belts), taking off on a makeshift runway hewn from packed clay and dirt was especially dangerous. Finally, there was always the factor of dangerous winter weather.[17]

On her second mission, the *Dakota Queen* blew her right-hand tire during take-off, but Lieutenant McGovern made the decision to continue the mission rather than abort. Both crew and the control tower were well aware that landing with only one functional wheel was quite dangerous, and, according to McGovern, "the tower officer gave me the option of bailing out or attempting a controlled landing when we returned." The stress of a potential crash landing was too much for engineer Mike Valko, a man who "had a temper that constantly got him into fistfights over seemingly minor provocations." In his 1977 autobiography, McGovern described Valko's reaction to the return flight: "He asked me countless times on the long flight back to the field if I really thought I could keep the plane from cartwheeling or skidding into a fiery crash. His face was contorted in fear and his hands were trembling. He desperately needed a drink—many drinks." McGovern landed the plane without injuries except for Valko's frayed nerves, which worsened over the course of future missions.[18]

During one of the crew's next flights, they fought for survival under the worst possible scenario. The *Dakota Queen* participated in a six-day offensive, the objective of which was the destruction of several strategic targets throughout Central and Eastern Europe, which included the railroad yards at Linz, Austria, the city of Hitler's birth. On the final day of the mission—a raid upon the Skoda Ammunition Works at Pilsen, Czechoslovakia—the *Dakota Queen*'s number two inboard engine failed. Although the crew was operating on three engines rather than four, they continued to the target.[19] As they positioned themselves for the bombing run, another engine failed. "The loss of oil pressure was so rapid that we were unable to feather the prop and it began windmilling," recalled McGovern in 1977.[20] At the time, the crew was over six hundred miles from the United States airbase at Cerignola.

The survival of those on board depended upon the calm cohesiveness of her crew, for the mistake of one could cost the lives of all. Evenly, crew commander McGovern made the decision to bring her home—which included bringing the B-24 down to six hundred feet on the shortest flight path homeward across the Adriatic. "I ordered everything in the plane to be thrown overboard to lighten the load," McGovern wrote of the incident, "—flak suits, ammunition, machine guns, oxygen tanks—everything that was loose or could be detached."[21] Then the unthinkable occurred. The plane "began vibrating fiercely," copilot Bill Rounds recalled. "We tried to feather it again but it wouldn't and just kept windmilling. We lost altitude rapidly and No. 3 burst into flame."[22] Due to the fact that the flames would burn through the B-24 engine's protective fire wall within five minutes and ignite the gasoline, plans to land in Italy were aborted. Rather than ditching the plane, however, McGovern descended and increased air speed to put out the flames and radioed the base that he was going to land the plane on the island of Vis rather than at Cerignola. The runway was less than half the length of the five thousand feet necessary to land a B-24 safely, but it was less than an hour away, and the only option left to the crew of the *Dakota Queen*.[23]

When the base came into view, the tower was notified of their predicament, and the pilots were instructed to maneuver the plane into the correct landing position. "As we turned onto that final approach," recalled McGovern, "we saw the wreckage of other planes that had overshot their landings and piled into a mountain at the far end of the little runway." While they were preparing for descent, the number three inboard engine caught fire once again. McGovern cut back on the gasoline, slowing the plane down for landing, which put the fire out. The pilot was well aware of the risk he had undertaken. "We knew that we had to hit that runway perfectly," he wrote, "and that there was no way to pull up and go around if we missed." From the moment the *Dakota Queen* touched ground, both pilot and copilot pushed the brakes to the floor of the cockpit, landing the plane without casualties. "The crew leaped out," McGovern remembered, "and literally kissed the ground."[24] Within a few moments, they watched in horror as a different B-24 missed the landing, hit the side of the mountain, and exploded. For engineer Mike Valko, it was more than his disposition could stand, and he was grounded for a few weeks in order to recuperate. For his steely determination and calm leadership that day, Second Lieutenant George McGovern won the Distinguished Flying Cross.[25]

As commander of a B-24 crew, McGovern was guided in his decisions by an unerring moral compass. Throughout his tour of duty, the young pilot relied upon the words of his father, who passed away of a heart attack while McGovern was in Europe. "You must learn to draw on the spiritual strength that is available to those who seek it," Reverend Joseph McGovern had told his son.[26] In January 1945, McGovern took the opportunity to attend a special audience for American servicemen with Pope Pius XII at the Vatican. Though of the Protestant faith, McGovern saw value in the blessing of the Holy Father in a time of war when moral sensibilities were easily violated. During one raid, for example, McGovern's crew had found their target obscured with a heavy overcast, forcing them to abort their mission. Air-force regulations stipulated that in such cases bombs should be disposed of in an uninhabited area, either over a large body of water or an open field. However, during that run a substitute navigator-bombadier intentionally dropped the *Dakota Queen's* explosives on a farmhouse. McGovern's waist gunner, William ("Tex") Ashlock, witnessed the act, confronted the bombardier, and brought the matter to McGovern's attention as crew commander. After cross-questioning the substitute about the incident, McGovern refused to fly with the bombardier again. Less than two weeks later, when weather curtailed a raid on an oil refinery at Moosbierbaum, Austria, all explosives on board the *Dakota Queen* were disposed of in a manner consistent with air-force regulations.[27]

The crew's final missions in late March and April 1945 were part of the Allies' grand strategy to destroy the Third Reich's ground transportation capabilities, making it nearly impossible for the Germans to move either men or materiel. Among the specific targets in this campaign were the Maribor rail bridge near the Austrian border in Yugoslavia (in this late stage of the war the only rail bridge over the Drava River) and the Saint Poelten rail yards on the Linz-Vienna rail line. During the initial twelve days of April, the crew of the *Dakota Queen* flew eleven missions. On the first day of April alone, twenty-seven B-24s dropped over seventy-eight tons of bombs. On 13 April, airmen at Cerignola received the news that Franklin Roosevelt had died, suffering a cerebral hemorrhage at Warm Springs, Georgia.[28] For the crew of the *Dakota Queen*, it was a blow. "Most of us had never really known the United States except with FDR as president," recalled McGovern. Roosevelt had "inspired all those who stood for freedom and decency in the war."[29] To these young fighting men in the midst of battle, it did not seem right that President Roosevelt had succumbed while Hitler still thrived. One disheartened officer proclaimed, "We've just lost the goddamn war."[30]

While the war was not lost, for McGovern and his crew the "toughest mission," the destruction of the railroad yards at Linz on 25 April 1945, was yet to come. "The anti-aircraft fire was amazingly heavy, concentrated and accurate," McGovern recalled of the event. "Our old B-24 was hit by more than a hundred pieces of shrapnel. Our hydraulic lines were severed in half a dozen places. The electrically heated suits that we wore to keep warm at subzero altitudes went cold and our oxygen supply was disrupted."[31] As McGovern said on another occasion, "Hell can't be any worse than that."[32] During this final mission, the *Dakota Queen* was slammed over and over with shrapnel and bounced around haphazardly as if tossed by a child. One piece of shrapnel hit gunner Ashlock, tearing through his leg from the knee into his buttocks, while another tore through the navigator's map. Behind and below formation, the aircraft began to lose altitude, and the pilots decided to return to Cerignola. They had no working brakes or flaps and a malfunctioning engine. As the plane approached home base, the crew was informed that they could ditch the plane in the Adriatic, bail out, or attempt to land. After a series of makeshift maneuvers, McGovern landed the *Dakota Queen* with only a few minor injuries among the crew. There was, however, one exception. Mike Valko collapsed mentally, spending the next few months in hospital for treatment of battle fatigue. Although his battle missions were now completed, McGovern acted as a pilot in relief efforts until he was finally shipped home with the members of his crew in June 1945.[33]

A Leader Tempered by War

The young pilot returned to a markedly different world. He came home to a wife with whom he had maintained a relationship only through correspondence that often took months to exchange and to a daughter he had seen only in photographs. The father he respected and admired was not there to greet him, along with many of his closest friends—casualties of war in so many ways. But more importantly, the experiences of war and ongoing events changed his perspective. McGovern concluded that the "nuclear monster" unleashed in August 1945 must be contained or the unchecked passions of man in war would destroy human civilization. Yet, he was not destined to play a merely passive role—the decorated former air-force pilot intended "to be a part of that postwar effort to build a structure of peace on the smoldering ruins of war."[34]

George McGovern was not the only American leader whose military experiences changed his views on war. A century earlier, Franklin Pierce, fourteenth president of the United States, had been a brigadier general during the Mexican-American War, commanding troops at the Battles of Contreras and Churubusco and the siege of Mexico City. The experience left a lasting impression on him. "I hate war in all its aspects," Pierce wrote later; "I deem it unworthy of the age in which I live."[35] In his opinion, victory on the battlefield was not a validation of any moral principle—only a demonstration of which side was more efficient and disciplined. Following his inauguration as president of the United States on 4 March 1853, Pierce exhausted every means at his disposal to prevent a civil war, including signing the Kansas-Nebraska Act in order to thwart Southern secession, at the cost of his political career. During the Civil War, Pierce was a highly vocal critic of President Abraham Lincoln's actions and policies, which, more than any other action of his public life, caused him to be treated like a traitor until his death on 8 October 1869.[36]

The aftereffects of war had much the same effect upon George McGovern as they had on Franklin Pierce over a century previous. From the beginning of his career in the United States Senate, McGovern lobbied for a negotiated settlement in Vietnam and the end of American involvement in Southeast Asia. In a speech before that body on 24 September 1963, the South Dakota senator predicted, "The trap we have fallen into there will haunt us in every corner of this revolutionary world if we do not properly appraise its lessons."[37] McGovern supported the resolution introduced by Idaho's senator Frank Church to cut off military and financial aid to South Vietnam. On 27 November 1965, he made a visit to Saigon, along with senators Mike Mansfield of Montana, Daniel Inouye of Hawaii, J. Caleb Boggs of Delaware, Edmund Muskie of Maine, and George Aiken of Vermont.[38] During the visit, McGovern toured an army hospital, and what he viewed there, in his own words, "answered any lingering doubts about the rightness of my opposition to the war":

> I met young Americans without legs, or arms, or faces, or genitals—all of them victims of land mines, booby traps or sniper fire. One handsome young lieutenant, his face twisted in pain, had just received a Purple Heart; both of his feet were missing. I was at a loss for words; I congratulated him for winning the Purple Heart. He looked at me and replied evenly, "Senator, that's easy to get in this damn place." We talked awhile about the war. He became the first of an endless stream of Vietnam veterans who were to tell me in the next few years of their disillusionment and disbelief.[39]

After that experience, Senator McGovern crossed the line from dissenter to crusader, determined "to do whatever might persuade the Congress and the American people to stop the horror."[40]

William McKinley, twenty-fifth president of the United States, who had served as a major and aide-de-camp to General Philip Sheridan during the American Civil War, had much the same response. Though outraged by Spain's treatment of Cuban colonials, McKinley was never in favor of another war as a solution, resisting nearly unanimous calls for unilateral military action even after the battleship *Maine* was sunk in Havana Harbor, purportedly by a Spanish mine. "I have been through one war," the president said. "I have seen the dead piled up, and I do not want to see another."[41]

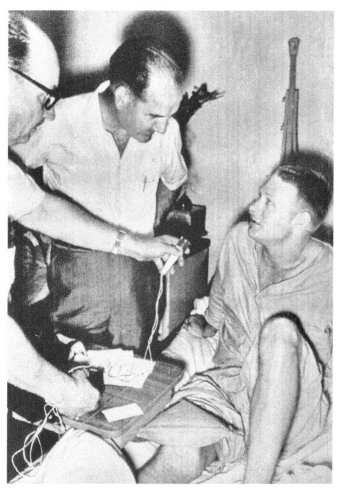

*Staff Sergeant Charles G. Wolff of Rapid City, South Dakota,
speaks with Senator McGovern and a newsman at the Third
Army Field Hospital in Saigon. UPI Radio photograph*

This attitude insulted many of McKinley's most ardent supporters, including his assistant secretary of the navy Theodore Roosevelt, who commented in disgust that the president had "no more
backbone than a chocolate éclair."[42] In the two months prior to the
outbreak of hostilities, President McKinley worked toward a peace
settlement with Spain and ultimately reached a tentative agreement. But, unlike Franklin Pierce, who sacrificed his career for
the sake of peace, McKinley bowed to the will of the expansion-
ists and warmongers. The president rejected the peace agreement
with Spain that had been negotiated under his auspices and asked
Congress for a declaration of war. Speaker of the House Joe Cannon said afterwards that McKinley "kept his ear so close to the
ground that it was full of grasshoppers."[43]

Like President McKinley, Senator McGovern submerged his
own revulsion for the war in Vietnam on one occasion to support
President Lyndon Johnson, casting a vote he described as "the one
I most regret during my public career."[44] Upon his elevation to
the presidency following John F. Kennedy's assassination, Johnson had authorized United States support for diversionary raids
in North Vietnam while the navy conducted a covert intelligence
mission in the Gulf of Tonkin. On 2 and 4 August 1964, the United
States battleship *Maddox* was attacked by North Vietnamese tor-
pedo boats; in reaction, President Johnson ordered immediate re-
taliatory air strikes and went before Congress to urge its support
for the escalation of the war.[45] What complicated matters was the
fact that 1964 was a presidential-election year and Johnson was
running for a term of his own; as a result, Democrats were rallying
around the president, even in delicate matters such as the height-
ening of American involvement in Vietnam. In the words of Arkansas senator J. William Fulbright, they wanted "to pull the rug
out from under [Republican nominee Barry] Goldwater."[46] Both
houses of Congress voted nearly unanimously to back the resolution on 7 August 1964.[47] Accepting Fulbright's assurance that
the Tonkin resolution was not a "blank check for war," McGovern
voted with the majority. "The lesson the Tonkin vote taught me,"
McGovern wrote in 1977, was "never to trade what I see as the
truth for a winking assurance in a back room."[48]

Conclusion

During the course of his thirty-five bombing missions in World War II, airman George McGovern learned that war should not be entered into without serious personal and national reflection. All peaceful means should first be thoroughly exhausted, and then the goals and perimeters of the conflict should be unmistakably defined. When violations of such objectives are brought to the attention of the nation, either the transgressors should be brought to justice in a timely manner or the conflagration brought to an end, either by negotiation or by abandonment. Senator McGovern consistently espoused these concepts throughout his entire political career, and they were the foundational principles of his 1972 presidential campaign.

Sadly, over 47 million voters did not listen. Americans rejected his positions and, in turn, allowed an ineffectual war to continue for three more years in the jungles of Vietnam. Yet, the history of that conflict has proven McGovern correct and, in the process, has mired the historical legacy of every president who was affected by it. It can be said that war taught much to students willing to take note of its lessons. In the case of George McGovern of Mitchell, South Dakota, the violence of war turned a young fighter pilot into a leader whose conscience and wisdom were his unerring moral compass.

NOTES

1. John F. Kennedy, Address to the Nation, 22 Oct. 1962, in *The Burden and the Glory: The Hopes and Purposes of President Kennedy's Second and Third Years in Office as Revealed in His Public Statements and Addresses*, ed. Allan Nevins (New York: Harper & Row, 1964), p. 96.

2. Leech, *In the Days of McKinley* (New York: Harper & Bros., 1959), p. 8.

3. Heckscher, *Woodrow Wilson: A Biography* (New York: Charles Scribner's Sons, 1991), p. 11.

4. Pierce, Diary, 25 July 1847, p. 51, in Franklin Pierce Papers, Manuscripts Division, Library of Congress, Washington, D.C., Presidential Papers Microfilm, 1959, Series 1, reel 1.

5. For a general overview of the costs and causes of World War II, *see* Loyd E. Lee, *World War II*, Greenwood Press Guides to Historic Events of the Twentieth Century (Westport, Conn.: Greenwood Press, 1999).

6. McGovern, *Grassroots: The Autobiography of George McGovern* (New York: Random House, 1977), p. 19.

7. Ibid.

8. Stephen E. Ambrose, *The Wild Blue: The Men and Boys Who Flew the B-24s over Germany* (New York: Simon & Schuster, 2001), pp. 31–33.

9. Ibid., pp. 43–46; McGovern, *Grassroots*, p. 18.

10. McGovern, *Grassroots*, pp. 22–23.

11. Ibid., p. 23.

12. Ambrose, *Wild Blue*, pp. 85–86, 96–104.

13. "Text of the Announcement" and "New American Air Force Bombs Messerschmitt Plant in Austria," *New York Times*, 3 Nov. 1943, pp. 1, 4; "Americans Bomb Turin and Genoa," ibid., 11 Nov. 1943, p. 6; "U-Boat Den Bombed," ibid., 25 Nov. 1943, p. 1; "Piraeus Battered by U.S. Bombers," ibid., 13 Jan. 1944, p. 5; "Toulon and Rome Bombed by Allies," ibid., 8 Mar. 1944, p. 1; "Rail Hubs Bombed," ibid., 18 Apr. 1944, p. 1. The Fifteenth Air Force was still part of the United States Army Air Forces; the United States Air Force was not established as a separate branch of the armed services until September 1947. Walter J. Boyne, *Beyond the Wild Blue: A History of the United States Air Force, 1947–1997* (New York: St. Martin's Press, 1997), pp. 365, 375; Carroll V. Glines, Jr., *The Compact History of the United States Air Force*, rev. ed. (New York: Hawthorn Books, 1973), pp. 232, 238.

14. Ambrose, *Wild Blue*, pp. 118, 153–60, 165.

15. Milton Bracker, "Bombing by Radar in B-17 Described," *New York Times*, 27 Nov. 1944, p. 5. Although the title specifically references a B-17 from the Eighth Air Force, the article discusses the Mickey radar at length and mentions the sites of McGovern's November mission, though without any revealing details.

16. McGovern, *Grassroots*, p. 26.

17. Ambrose, *Wild Blue*, pp. 175–77. Of the weight problem, a crew chief said: "If you don't like it, what do you want to leave behind? Machine gun ammunition? The flak suits? Take less gasoline? Or what? You're going to have to take the bombs or there is no point in going" (quoted ibid., p. 176).

18. McGovern, *Grassroots*, pp. 25–26. In Ambrose's *Wild Blue*, pp. 187–88, the story of this mission is slightly different, and it occurs as the third or fourth mission of the *Dakota Queen*.

19. "15th Air Force Bombs Austria and Germany," *New York Times*, 21 Dec. 1944, p. 4; Ambrose, *Wild Blue*, p. 192.

20. McGovern, *Grassroots*, p. 27.

21. Ibid.

22. Quoted in Ambrose, *Wild Blue*, p. 192.

23. Ibid., pp. 192–94.

24. McGovern, *Grassroots*, p. 27.

25. Ibid.; Ambrose, *Wild Blue*, pp. 194–96.

26. Quoted in McGovern, *Grassroots*, p. 29.

27. Ambrose, *Wild Blue*, pp. 205–6, 208–9.

28. "Day-Long Bombings Rake across Reich" and "Brenner Pass Line Again Ripped," *New York Times*, 1 Apr. 1945, p. 4; "15th Again Rips Rails ahead of Red Army," *New York Times*, 2 Apr. 1945, p. 6; Ambrose, *Wild Blue*, p. 237; Jim Bishop, *FDR's Last Year: April 1944–April 1945* (New York: William Morrow & Co., 1974), pp. 531–90.

29. McGovern, *Grassroots*, p. 29.

30. Quoted ibid.

31. Ibid., p. 28.

32. Quoted in Ambrose, *Wild Blue*, p. 241.

33. Ibid., pp. 241–45, 256; McGovern, *Grassroots*, pp. 27–28.

34. McGovern, *Grassroots*, pp. 30–31.

35. Pierce, Diary, 25 July 1847, p. 51.

36. Roy Franklin Nichols, *Franklin Pierce: Young Hickory of the Granite Hills* (Philadelphia: University of Pennsylvania Press, 1931), pp. 522–23, 526–27, 532.

37. McGovern, *Grassroots*, p. 97.

38. "Why Help Vietnam?," *New York Times*, 13 Sept. 1963, p. 25; Charles Mohr, "Senator McGovern Reassured in Saigon on Strong U.S. Drive," ibid., 3 Dec. 1965, p. 6.

39. McGovern, *Grassroots*, p. 107.

40. Ibid. For more on McGovern's subsequent actions, *see* Daryl Webb, "Crusade: George McGovern's Opposition to the Vietnam War," *South Dakota History* 28 (Fall 1998): 161–90.

41. Quoted in Edmund Morris, *The Rise of Theodore Roosevelt* (New York: Coward, McCann & Geoghegan, 1979), p. 600.

42. Roosevelt, quoted in Leech, *In the Days of McKinley*, p. 169.

43. Quoted in Paul F. Boller, Jr., *Presidential Anecdotes* (New York: Oxford University Press, 1981), p. 191.

44. McGovern, *Grassroots*, p. 103.

45. Robert S. McNamara, with Brian VanDeMark, *In Retrospect: The Tragedy and Lessons of Vietnam* (New York: Times Books, 1995), pp. 129–35.

46. Quoted in McGovern, *Grassroots*, p. 103.

47. "Congress Backs President on Southeast Asia Moves; Khanh Sets State of Siege," *New York Times*, 8 Aug. 1964, pp. 1–2. Of President John-

son's willingness to escalate the Vietnam War after his reelection, Senator McGovern stated, "I was filled with sadness and foreboding that this powerful, well-meaning man who wanted so desperately to be a great President was heading down the road to disaster" (*Grassroots*, p. 105).

48. McGovern, *Grassroots*, p. 104.

CHAPTER THREE

FROM THE GRASSROOTS

BUILDING THE SOUTH DAKOTA

DEMOCRATIC PARTY

VALERIE R. O'REGAN AND

STEPHEN J. STAMBOUGH

 It is safe to say that the South Dakota Democratic Party has had its share of ups and downs. During the down years, South Dakota could be viewed as a one-party state—that party being the Republican party. But there have also been years when the state Democratic party has succeeded in capturing some of the key seats in the state and at the national level. These success stories include Governor and Senator William J. Bulow, Governor Tom Berry, Governor Ralph Herseth, Governor Richard Kneip, Senator Tom Daschle, Senator Tim Johnson, and, of course, Senator and presidential nominee George McGovern. Since the mid-1950s, the Democratic party has fought its way to a respectable presence in the state and has provided significant representation at the national level. One person has been credited with this revitalization of the Democratic party of South Dakota; that person is George McGovern. Almost single-handedly, McGovern turned the party around so that the citizens of the state continue to have a choice of political parties and candidates.[1]

The South Dakota Democratic Party to 1953

Despite its noted "populist" tendencies, South Dakota is a conservative state. The conservative slant is not limited to the Republican party; many consider South Dakota's Democratic party to be conservative in comparison to the national norm. Despite this conservative inclination, the Democrats of South Dakota have succeeded in differentiating themselves from Republicans, but becoming a competitive force has been harder for them. Republican dominance is nothing unusual in a state that Neal R. Peirce labels "a state of reluctant change."[2] Throughout the years, Republicans have controlled the state legislature and statehouse with only periodic victories by the Democrats. National-level congressional seats have also been consistently filled by Republicans, but here Democrats have made more progress.

Throughout the late nineteenth and early twentieth centuries, the South Dakota Democratic Party had limited success at the polls. For a short time in the 1890s, the Democrats joined forces with the Populists to provide a somewhat successful opposition to the Republicans, electing fusionist governor Andrew E. Lee in 1896. With the split of these two divergent parties in 1900 came the return of Republican party preeminence until 1926, when a conservative Democrat, William J. Bulow, won the governor's seat. For the next two election cycles, the Democrats' presence in the state legislature ebbed and flowed. The Democrats lost the governor's seat in 1930, but gained a United States Senate seat when Bulow was elected to the Senate. A high point for the South Dakota Democratic Party occurred during the 1932 elections when the Democrats won control of the state legislature, the statewide offices, and the two national-level House seats. Governor Tom Berry and the other Democratic winners continued this success through the 1934 elections. However, the victory was short-lived as the Republicans rebounded in 1936, taking back the governor's seat and one of the congressional seats; by 1938, the Republicans once again dominated the state offices, the state legislature, and the two congressional seats.[3]

Republican party dominance during the time period from 1938 to 1954 has been attributed to the extremely liberal orientation of the national Democratic party and to the lack of appealing state Democratic candidates in South Dakota. During this period, support for the Democratic party declined to the point that some counties had no party leadership or organization. In 1952, with the Republicans winning handsomely at the national level, the South Dakota Republican Party was at the pinnacle of its partisan strength throughout the state. During that election, only two Democrats were elected to the state house of representatives, and the state senate became a one-party chamber. In addition, Republicans held all four national-level congressional seats as well as the

governor's office. The state had become one of the most noncom-
petitive (by party) in the nation. The utter failure of the Democratic party statewide during this time concerned some political
leaders nationally and worried many South Dakotans.[4]

Enter McGovern and His Two-Party Dream

George McGovern became the executive secretary of the Democratic party in South Dakota in 1953, following the Republican
landslide in the 1952 elections. South Dakota newspaperman Les
Helgeland noted that McGovern took over "at a time when you
couldn't call it a party in South Dakota—at a time when the Democrats had only two members in the 110-member legislature." As
a result, when the "tall, slender, softspoken party secretary made
his stops in Pierre," the Republicans considered him a "spy."[5] Mc-
Govern's assumption of the office marked the first time that the
state party had had a full-time organizer, and his primary responsibility was to shape the party into a competitive political institution. The new secretary recognized the need to establish a viable
party and understood the benefits of a stronger and more expan-
sive organization to his own future.[6]

Despite the impressive title of executive secretary, the position held few initial benefits, negligible resources, and no clear
duties. McGovern had to generate the funds for his own salary;
something that was not easy to do in a state where grassroots
and state party organization were almost nonexistent. His solution was to establish the Century Club, a fund-raising strategy
in which people contributed one hundred dollars per year. This
money covered McGovern's salary and travel expenses and established a toehold for the struggling party in the state. The Century
Club is still a primary source of funding for South Dakota's Democratic party.[7]

South Dakota is a large state geographically, with few urban
areas. As a result, McGovern spent a substantial amount of time
on the road, driving from town to town. In the process, he educated himself about the concerns of the populace, meeting with
the remaining party faithful to collect the information necessary
to rebuild party leadership and membership. When there was no
one to meet—some towns had no Democratic leaders and no

McGovern gave up his position as a faculty member at Dakota Wesleyan University to serve as executive director of South Dakota's Democratic party.

one with experience in Democratic politics—McGovern gathered the information on his own, identifying possible county officers and workers in such communities. As he gathered names, contacts, and other useful personal information, McGovern documented each contact on a three-by-five note card, accumulating a catalogue of Democratic supporters. This inauspicious start was typical of the days before electronic information-management systems, but the cards collected during McGovern's tenure as executive secretary literally helped rejuvenate the Democratic party while forming a valuable resource for his own future political endeavors.[8]

As McGovern became more familiar with the condition of the party throughout the state and the gradually expanding party membership, his trips were transformed into crusades to reach out to all South Dakotans, not just Democrats. McGovern realized that for a Democrat to win in South Dakota, the candidate needed to appeal to members of both parties as well as to independents.[9] To the young politician, the prospect of attracting a broad coalition of supporters across the state was an appealing goal and one for which he was well suited. "McGovern's deliberate and open style of exchanging ideas with others" won friends and impressed rivals, political observer Herb Cheever noted. "South Dakota voters valued McGovern's principles because he frequently showed he valued theirs."[10] His years as minister and educator had prepared him well for these personal exchanges on the back roads of South Dakota. Furthermore, the road trips were useful for recruiting viable candidates for upcoming state and county elections.

This grassroots approach transformed the Democratic party and its efforts. Unlike later media-driven campaigns to build party support, McGovern's efforts assured a viable and relatively stable base of support. The personal touch McGovern used to save the two-party system in South Dakota was so effective that, incredibly, during the 1954 state elections, Democrats took six of the senate seats and eighteen of the house seats. Although Republicans still retained all the statewide offices in the next election two years later, that pivotal and historic ballot further expanded the Democrats' presence in the state legislature. During the 1956 elections, the number of Democrats in the state senate and state house increased to seventeen and twenty-seven, respectively.[11] The increase in the state senate allowed Democrats to come within one seat of controlling that body. Moreover, that year McGovern became the first South Dakota Democrat since 1936 to win election to a national-level office by capturing one of the state's two congressional seats. In a remarkably short period of time, McGovern's dream of providing South Dakotans with viable political choices in a two-party system had become a reality. It also launched McGovern's political star, positioning him for what was to become a long and noteworthy career in politics.[12]

The Party-Building Legacy Continues

After the rebuilding of the South Dakota Democratic Party in the mid-1950s, three questions still needed to be answered. First, would McGovern's success extend to victories for a variety of offices rather than for just a few based upon individual personalities? Second, would the successes be just short-term gains, much like the brief successes in the 1930s? Third, would future successes be defined simply as occasional victories or would the Democratic party be strong enough to hold the Republicans accountable, playing its role in a true two-party system?

As Table 1 and Figure 1 make abundantly clear, substantial gains were made by Democrats at all levels in 1954 and beyond, answering the first question. The first two columns in Table 1 show the percentage of the vote for each level of statewide office and the level of representation in the state legislative chambers. The remarkable degree of success demonstrated immediately after McGovern took over party organization could not be attributed to just one or two dazzling personalities that captured the imagination of a small segment of the voters. The general improvement in electoral success by Democrats could be seen at every level.

This multilevel success was important for two reasons. First, the impressive improvement in such a short period of time served as a powerful recruiting tool for future supporters, volunteers, contributors, and everything else needed to sustain a political party. Second, by electing more state senators and state representatives, the party was creating a larger pool of qualified and experi-

TABLE I: *Levels of Voter Support for Democrats Before and After McGovern's Party-Building*

Office	1952 Election	1954 Election	Pre-McGovern	Post-McGovern	Significance
Governor	29.80%	43.30%	37.56%	44.54%	**
Secretary of State	31.90%	41.00%	34.35%	43.44%	***
State Auditor	31.90%	42.50%	33.92%	42.36%	**
State Treasurer	32.20%	43.70%	34.58%	45.39%	***
Attorney General	33.40%	44.60%	34.77%	40.65%	N.S.
Percentage of Seats in State House of Representatives	2.67%	24.00%	15.18%	31.53%	***
Percentage of Seats in State Senate	0%	17.14%	19.98%	37.02%	***

Statistical significance based upon t-tests for Pre- and Post-McGovern era

***< .01 level of significance

**< .05 level of significance

Sources for table and figures: Data up to 1968 are from Alan L. Clem, *South Dakota Political Almanac*, 2d ed. (Vermillion, S.Dak.: Dakota Press, 1969). More recent data were compiled by Rich Braunstein, University of South Dakota, Vermillion.

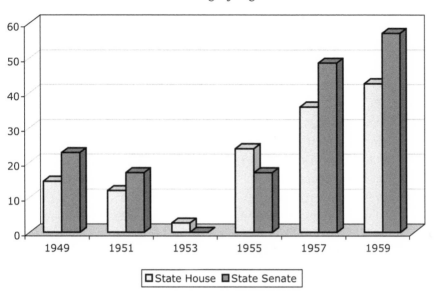

FIGURE 1: *Democratic Percentage of Legislative Chambers*

□State House ■State Senate

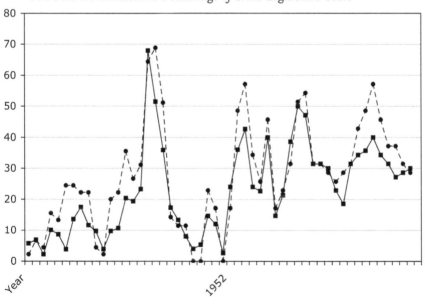

FIGURE 2: *Democratic Percentage of State Legislative Seats*

—■—State House − − ●− − State Senate

enced candidates to run for higher office eventually. This larger pool of qualified candidates was crucial if the party was to maintain its gains and expand on them at higher levels in future years.

The next question that needed to be answered was whether the hard work during the early 1950s would become institutionalized into long-term party success. An examination of Table 1 and Figures 2 and 3 suggests that the hard work would not be wasted. There is a clear difference between the level of electoral success before and after the 1953 period. As illustrated in Figures 2 and 3, the fortunes of the South Dakota Democratic Party did wax and wane throughout the years, but they never declined to the previous low levels when the party was nearly nonexistent.

Further support is found by comparing the numbers in the last two columns of Table 1, where there is a substantive increase in the level of support for statewide candidates in the post-McGovern party-building era. This increase averaged approximately eight percentage points for all the races, and the difference attained statistical significance for all offices except that of state attorney general. Although these numbers indicate that the Democratic party is still the minority party in the state, a sustained increase of that magnitude means that the party is now in a position to win when they recruit well and manage good campaigns and when national or regional partisan tides favor them. That last fact, perhaps, is the greatest impact of a stable infrastructure. While there will be— and there were—down years in terms of party success, the infrastructure established by McGovern makes it possible for the party to win when fortunes turn their way. They are able to take full advantage of favorable issues, trends, and human resources. Without a sufficient infrastructure, many of these opportunities would be lost.

Finally, for the McGovern legacy as party builder to be secure, the Democratic party also needs to have enough support to serve as the loyal opposition when fortunes favor the Republicans. Without a significant minority party holding the majority accountable, democracy does not work. McGovern, the scholar, knew that; McGovern, the activist, knew that, too. The findings reported in Table 1 speak to this issue, as well. Not only was there a significant

FIGURE 3: *Average Percentage of Vote for Statewide Democratic Candidates*

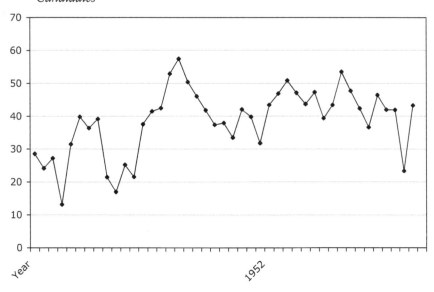

Offices included are governor, secretary of state, state auditor, attorney general, and state treasurer. In 1998, there were no Democratic candidates for attorney general and state auditor, greatly decreasing the overall average.

increase in the level of support from the pre-1953 period to the post-1953 period, but the level that was obtained also reached some important numbers. By moving the average support for most of these offices from the mid-30 percent level to the mid-40 percent level, South Dakota Democrats moved into the range of competitive elections. Generally, a seat is considered to be safe for one party if the normal party margin of victory is beyond the 55–45 percent range. Due to the 10 percent increase, the party finally moved from electoral obscurity to the edges of competitiveness in many more elections. Further, the party practically doubled their normal level of representation in the legislature. The increased number of partisans made it possible for networks to form, agendas to be forwarded, and the party structure to survive.

Obviously, however, much work needs to be done for the continued health of the South Dakota Democratic Party. The fact that the numbers presented in Table 1 are considered a success is telling, both of how dismal the party prospects were when George McGovern took over and of how much work still needs to be done. Usually, political parties are not happy with an average of 30 to 40 percent representation in the legislature; nor are they accepting of approximately 40 to 45 percent of the vote in an average statewide election. Although it is a tremendous improvement over the previous era, if the South Dakota Democratic Party wants to expand on what McGovern built, it will have to focus on the next level of competitiveness.

The foundation built fifty years ago was strong enough to develop and sustain a two-party system in South Dakota for the first time in its history. It was strong enough to produce another generation of political leaders like the current United States Senate delegation, which includes Tom Daschle, the leader of the Democratic party nationally (including his tenure as Senate majority leader). However, if a modern-day George McGovern were to assume the task of party-builder today, the goal would be to move past the role of a competitive loyal opposition and into the role of a governing party. In accomplishing that task, such a leader would benefit from the fact that the foundation for such an objective had already been laid by George McGovern.

NOTES

1. Alan L. Clem, *Prairie State Politics: Popular Democracy in South Dakota* (Washington, D.C.: Public Affairs Press, 1967), p. 55.

2. Peirce, *The Great Plains States of America: People, Politics, and Power in the Nine Great Plains States* (New York: W. W. Norton & Co., 1972), p. 174.

3. Terrence J. Lindell, "Populists in Power: The Problems of the Andrew E. Lee Administration in South Dakota," *South Dakota History* 22 (Winter 1992): 345–48; Alan L. Clem, *South Dakota Political Almanac*, 2d ed. (Vermillion, S.Dak.: Dakota Press, 1969), pp. 18, 26, 48–52.

4. Clem, *Prairie State Politics*, pp. 11, 38–41; Robert Sam Anson, *McGovern: A Biography* (New York: Holt, Rinehart & Winston, 1972), pp. 69–73; Clem, *South Dakota Political Almanac*, p. 59.

5. Helgeland, quoted in *Pierre Daily Capital Journal*, 17 July 1972.

6. Anson, *McGovern*, pp. 66–67, 74; McGovern, *Grassroots: The Autobiography of George McGovern* (New York: Random House, 1977), p. 51.

7. Anson, *McGovern*, p. 67; McGovern, *Grassroots*, pp. 57–58.

8. McGovern, *Grassroots*, pp. 57–58.

9. Anson, *McGovern*, pp. 73–74; McGovern, *Grassroots*, p. 57.

10. Cheever, quoted in Rick Hauffe, "McGovern Is Natural Leader," *South Dakota Hall of Fame* 20 (Fall 1994): 28.

11. Clem, *South Dakota Political Almanac*, p. 26.

12. For more on McGovern's early political career and other factors affecting the 1954 and 1956 elections, *see* Jon K. Lauck, "George S. McGovern and the Farmer: South Dakota Politics, 1953–1962," *South Dakota History* 32 (Winter 2002): 331–41.

CHAPTER FOUR

CONGRESSIONAL EXPERIENCES,

CONGRESSIONAL LEGACIES

GARY AGUIAR

 George McGovern's congressional experiences showcased his lifelong political commitment to fighting hunger and military interventionism. Perhaps most notably in McGovern's twenty-two-year congressional career, he served as a vocal advocate for reining in the military-industrial complex about which President Dwight D. Eisenhower warned. Even though McGovern's advocacy failed to reduce military spending, his legislative efforts did lead to more food for poor families worldwide. And even though he was unable to construct majorities in Congress to support his most "radical" proposals, the central core of his congressional proposals later served as the foundation for his presidential campaigns.

Much of McGovern's efforts in Congress revolved around his concern that military spending, which comprised half of the federal budget, was wasteful and misdirected. His overriding goal was to redirect those federal dollars to more efficacious programs and objectives, especially the ending of hunger around the world. Interestingly, McGovern biographer Robert Sam Anson argues that McGovern's desire to reduce military waste was a conservative philosophy that safeguarded taxpayers' dollars by directing them to more productive uses.[1] Unlike many public figures, McGovern possessed the remarkable ability to develop cohesive policies on global issues and communicate their relevance to ordinary citizens. Certainly, a reliance on his strong Christian values helped him win support among mostly conservative South Dakotans. In short, his twin goals of reducing the role of the military and promoting programs to solve social ills guided McGovern's congressional career, in which, for the most part, he successfully married his electoral experiences to his policy preferences.

Campaigns for Congress

Wind-swept South Dakota is a conservative, Republican state. Other than a brief dalliance with populism in the early part of the twentieth century, fiscal conservatism has reigned supreme. Moreover, Republicans have dominated the state's history from statehood to the present. Yet, under McGovern's leadership, South Dakota Democrats had some significant successes in the 1950s and 60s. McGovern's ideals of leadership were, like those of many other liberals in the 1950s, inspired by Adlai Stevenson's leadership in revitalizing the Democratic party nationally.[2]

As a keen student of politics, McGovern knew that he faced long odds every time he ran for public office in South Dakota. He spent several years building the South Dakota Democratic Party, and the contacts, experiences, and skills he developed paved the way for his first campaign in 1956, when he sought a seat in the United States House of Representatives. On a larger scale, McGovern's ability to reshape the terms of the debate and campaign exhaustively for votes led to many victories not only for himself but for other Democrats around the state.[3]

In 1956, South Dakota's first congressional district was represented by Harold Lovre, a four-term incumbent who had grown complacent. McGovern beat Lovre to become the first Democrat that South Dakotans sent to Washington, D.C., in nearly a quarter of a century. His election to the United States House was built on a combination of factors. First, in 1954, a strong challenger in the Republican primary had softened up Lovre's support. Also, McGovern's party-building efforts had led to substantial name recognition in the congressional district, and his argument that the state required a strong two-party system appealed to independents and some disaffected Republicans. Finally, McGovern put long hours into working the back roads of rural South Dakota that state Republicans had long neglected.[4]

Two years later, popular former governor Joe Foss, an ace World War II pilot, challenged McGovern for the congressional seat, but Foss had not learned the lessons of the 1956 campaign. While Mc-

Govern continued to beat the bushes in rural areas, Foss relied on the state Republican party organization to generate votes in the state's larger communities. McGovern, a strong defender of the family farmer, cemented his victory by positioning himself as a vocal critic of the Eisenhower Administration's agricultural policies, which had substantially reduced crop subsidies.[5]

By 1960, McGovern, unsatisfied with his role in the House, desired a more visible platform for his ideas. This move was not surprising given McGovern's success, ambition, and the fact that, like other members of the lower chamber from small states, South Dakota congressmen have been more likely to run for the Senate than those from larger states. As a junior member of a large chamber, McGovern was denied access to the national media in showcasing his ideas. To achieve his aim, McGovern took on a legendary figure in South Dakota politics, the long-time senator and "red-baiter" Karl Mundt, but McGovern's hatred for Mundt's aggressive, overly simplistic anti-Communism clouded his strategy. Thus, McGovern's first loss for electoral office might be seen, in part, as a failed attempt to hurry history. Another factor in the defeat was McGovern's support of John F. Kennedy's 1960 presidential bid. After the election, Robert Kennedy concluded that his brother had cost McGovern a Senate seat in South Dakota and, in 1961, convinced President Kennedy to appoint McGovern as director of the languishing Food for Peace Program. For almost two years, McGovern's two political passions were united as he expanded the program to use agricultural surpluses to feed the world and promote peace through nonmilitary strategies.[6]

In 1962, McGovern planned to challenge Senator Francis Case for South Dakota's other Senate seat when Case unexpectedly died in June. The Republican party nominated Lieutenant Governor Joe Bottum to replace Case on the ticket. Anson argues that Bottum was the weakest of the seven potential Republicans for the nomination, allowing McGovern to emerge as the favored candidate. However, McGovern was struck by hepatitis in the last weeks of the campaign, and his wife Eleanor campaigned on his behalf. McGovern won by a tiny margin, one of the closest statewide races in South Dakota history. Newly elected Senator McGovern now

As an advocate for his agrarian constituents, Congressman McGovern spent time listening to the concerns of fellow South Dakotans.

possessed the platform he desired to broadcast his ideas to a national audience.[7]

In 1968, McGovern briefly sought the Democratic presidential nomination, mostly to hold Robert Kennedy's delegates together after the latter's assassination. McGovern severely criticized the police treatment of protestors at Chicago's legendarily divisive Democratic National Convention that year. Some weeks later, however, he met with Mayor Richard Daley of Chicago and suggested the possibility that only a few officers had overstepped their bounds. McGovern's uncharacteristic backpedaling on the issue did little to help him with either side. At the Democratic National Convention, he had also endorsed the nomination of his long-time friend Hubert Humphrey but not Humphrey's approach to the Vietnam War, which mirrored that of the Lyndon B. Johnson Administration.[8]

After the convention, McGovern returned home to the State Fair in Huron and received an enthusiastic welcome from massive crowds. At the same time, his bid for reelection to the Senate was not to be the simple battle he had anticipated, as his large lead in the polls early in the spring had dematerialized into a dead heat by the time of the Democratic convention. McGovern possessed some key advantages in this first Senate reelection bid: he was the incumbent, and he enjoyed celebrity status as potential presidential timber. While Archie Gubbrud, a conservative former governor, appeared to be a strong challenger, he was an inarticulate, noncommittal speaker who ran an unusually negative campaign. In the end, Gubbrud's attack strategy backfired; South Dakotans tend to punish campaigners who engage in negative advertising. Moreover, Gubbrud's disorganized campaign was ineffective at the grassroots. In contrast, the hard campaigning of a superb McGovern organization, bolstered by busloads of out-of-state college students, combined with the candidate's personal charm to win him reelection by a wider margin than his initial Senate election.[9]

During the next four years, McGovern, with his sights set on a presidential run in 1972, built a national reputation as an opponent of the Vietnam War. At mid-century, the United States Senate operated as an incubator for presidential candidates, especially risk-takers like McGovern. To neutralize other senators, McGovern unveiled a new approach to presidential campaigns by announcing his candidacy early and campaigning extensively, making numerous visits to college campuses across the country. Even to the present day, McGovern is often credited with initiating what has become a staple of presidential campaigns.[10]

Ironically, McGovern's loss to Richard Nixon in the 1972 presidential race made his 1974 Senate reelection campaign much less formidable. Leftover funds and new contributors meant the latter effort was flush with campaign monies, which McGovern admits may have been squandered. While former Vietnam POW Leo Thorsness presented a strong challenge, events certainly were in McGovern's favor in 1974. Watergate, particularly Richard Nixon's resignation, boosted McGovern's prospects. Also, he was the second-ranking Democrat on the Senate Agriculture Committee and regularly reminded the state's voters that he was next in line to be chair.[11] McGovern won.

In 1980, McGovern's long congressional tenure ended with a loss to Representative James Abdnor. McGovern was among a handful of liberal senators targeted by the National Conservative Political Action Committee, and he therefore faced withering and well-funded criticism in his home state. The unpopularity of President Jimmy Carter also contributed to the loss. Furthermore, Abdnor's claim that McGovern had lost touch with his constituents may have struck a chord with the state's more conservative voters.[12] "It's remarkable," McGovern told a reporter, "that as a liberal Democrat I stayed in office as long as I did in what is essentially a conservative state."[13]

Throughout his congressional career, George McGovern won elections by conceptualizing his constituents as peaceful Christian agriculturalists. He built strong bridges to family farmers and perhaps also invigorated a latent pacifist streak. Certainly no isolationist, McGovern argued that the United States should foster strong relationships with nascent democrats—not anti-Communist dictators—around the world. In his communication with constituents, McGovern emphasized his twin issues. For example, more than two-thirds of the articles in his constituency newsletters in 1963 through 1965 focused on agriculture and foreign policy. During that period, the other members of South Dakota's congressional delegation highlighted these issues in less than half of the articles in their newsletters. Like other successful legislators, he heeded constituency preferences on domestic issues but was free to pursue other cues on foreign policy.[14]

Committees and Legislation

Committees are the central institution for the production of legislation in Congress. McGovern sought membership on committees that would further his work on international affairs and agricultural issues. As a senator, he served on both the agriculture and interior committees and rose to chair the latter's Indian affairs subcommittee in 1967. In the 1960s, McGovern was unable to secure a seat on the highly prized Senate Foreign Affairs Committee because Senate rules prevented two senators from one state from serving on the same major committee and Mundt was already a member. After Mundt's retirement in 1972, McGovern finally gained a seat on foreign affairs and dropped his interior committee assignment. In a daring bit of legislative maneuvering, McGovern created and chaired the Senate Select Committee on Nutrition and Human Needs from 1967 to 1978. While both the Senate's agriculture and rules committees opposed his effort to establish and fund the select committee, McGovern won a victory over his party's leadership by taking his fight directly to the Senate floor.[15]

In agricultural policy, McGovern focused on programs that provided food for the hungry, both at home and worldwide. His select committee showcased the lack of proper nutrition among poor Americans, and he successfully fought for the expansion of food-stamp and school-lunch programs. He played a pivotal role in the principle of free lunches to the poorest children in the country. As a member of the House, McGovern had worked with Hubert Humphrey to transform Public Law 480, a weak trade-assistance law, into the Food for Peace Program.[16]

McGovern frequently attempted to combine his twin issues. For example, in his first year in the Senate, he proposed a 10 percent across-the-board cut in military spending to fund a tax cut and redirect funds to domestic programs. He also introduced a national economic conversion bill that would begin planning for the movement of resources from military to civilian production. Clearly, his most visible efforts emphasized a more peaceful approach to international relations. In a now-famous speech on the Senate floor in 1963, McGovern was the first senator to criticize the use of the military in Vietnam. He had earlier opposed the Eisenhower Doctrine, which authorized presidential action in the Middle East, as an unconstitutional usurpation of congressional powers. However, McGovern did vote with his party's president for the Gulf of Tonkin Resolution, which gave President Johnson authority to expand the war in Vietnam. Almost immediately, he regretted that vote, and not long after Johnson's landslide victory in 1964, McGovern strongly criticized the administration's foreign policy in a Senate speech that caught the nation's attention.[17]

Nevertheless, McGovern was relatively late among Senate "doves" to break with the president on Vietnam. Although his philosophy argued for negotiations with North Vietnam, he wanted to maintain open lines of communication with the administration. But by 1965, McGovern saw President Johnson's approach as fruitless. In some ways, McGovern, like other politicians, was greatly influenced by events of the turbulent sixties. He became a vocal symbol of the antiwar movement by advocating immediate withdrawal of troops from Vietnam. McGovern's personal crusade against the war in southeast Asia was furthered when *Life* magazine brought the conflict home to ordinary Americans in July 1969 by publishing the photographs of servicemen who had died in the fighting. McGovern used the occasion for another Senate speech against the war, and many prominent senators rose to praise his antiwar efforts. In 1970, he introduced the Amendment to End the War by cutting off funds for the war effort. This so-called McGovern-Hatfield Amendment to the Military Procurement Authorization Act was bolstered by a McGovern-inspired half-hour televised program that discussed the war and generated enough monies to fund the Committee to End the War, which lobbied Congress. The proposal died, but it received thirty-nine "yea" votes, including those of a majority of the Senate's Democrats.[18]

McGovern relied primarily on legislative efforts to end the war, eschewing more radical means of political action. For instance,

the senator participated in only one peace march and was openly
worried about the dangerous radicals of the Left, who regularly engaged in violent behavior. However, he did not limit his activities
to the Senate floor; he made many speeches to college audiences
at the height of the antiwar movement and always concluded each
speech with a popular question-and-answer session. His efforts to
negotiate peace were almost certainly hampered by his landslide
loss in 1972. After his presidential defeat, McGovern concentrated
his efforts around his new assignment on the Senate Foreign Affairs Committee. Here he attempted to find peaceable solutions
in several global hotspots, including Cuba, the Korean Peninsula,
and the Mideast.[19]

How successful was McGovern in transforming his Senate seat
into a national platform for his ideas? One way to track the visibility of politicians is to map the extent of their media coverage.
Figure 1 graphs the number of articles that refer to McGovern in
the *New York Times* from 1957 to 1980. As a junior member of the
House of Representatives and director of the Food for Peace Program, McGovern received little attention from the national press.
In his first term in the Senate, he received only slightly more attention but still less than three dozen references through 1967.
This lack of coverage is typical for South Dakota senators because
of the state's small population, geographic location, and agricultural character. For example, Senator Francis Case (R-SD), who
served in the Senate from 1951 to 1962, was virtually invisible to
the national media. Similarly, Senator James Abourezk (D-SD),
who served from 1973 to 1980, received only several dozen references per year. Even Senator Karl Mundt (R-SD), who served in
Congress for thirty-four years, received poor coverage from the national media. During this period, the *New York Times* published
only about a dozen articles per year that refer to him.

As Figure 1 notes, this pattern is consistent with the coverage of other midwestern senators. For example, Senator Walter
Mondale (D-MN), who served from 1964 to 1976, did not gar-
ner much national attention either. Mondale received only about
one hundred *New York Times* references per year well into his
second term. Similarly, Senator Eugene McCarthy (D-MN) was
barely mentioned in the *Times* until 1968, when he challenged a

sitting president for his party's nomination. In 1968, McCarthy remained a viable candidate at the fractured Chicago convention and received more than one thousand mentions in the *New York Times*. However, his totals dropped rapidly in the following years.

McGovern began to receive significant national attention in 1968, coinciding with his bid for the Democratic presidential nomination, when the *Times* referenced him 163 times. However, McGovern's visibility increased substantially in the following years; by 1972, he received more than nine hundred *New York Times* references. Moreover, he continued to receive substantial coverage for several years after he lost his presidential bid. Much of this latter coverage was related to his ideas, which resonated with the era. In short, McGovern made an impression on the national consciousness that went beyond his presidential candidacy.

Voting Patterns

McGovern's presidential bid clearly affected his national visibility and gave exposure to his ideas, but to what extent did the exposure and his presidential ambitions affect his behavior in Congress? Studies suggest that in the period from 1959 to 1980 ideology was the single most important factor in explaining roll-call votes. Another study suggests that among United States senators in 1967, McGovern was closely linked to a bloc of liberal senators on civil-rights issues. However, he was only weakly linked to the liberal voting bloc on foreign and defense policies.[20] Did his presidential campaigns alter his voting patterns on recorded votes on the chamber floor? These votes, reported by *Congressional Quarterly* (*CQ*), are essential to understanding legislators' behaviors because members of Congress recognize the public nature of these votes. *CQ* analyzes all recorded votes in Congress in annual almanacs.

First, to what extent did McGovern participate in Senate votes? Figure 2 graphs voting participation—listed as the proportion of times a senator casts votes on roll-call votes—for McGovern and other Senate Democrats. Early in his Senate career, McGovern outscored his chamber colleagues by participating in nearly 90 percent of all roll-call votes on the Senate floor. However, on four occasions his voting participation dropped below two-thirds

FIGURE 1: *References in New York Times for Selected Senators,*
1957–1980

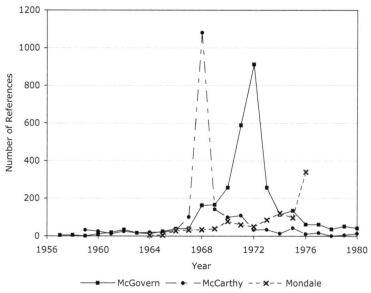

Source: *New York Times Index,* 1957–1980

FIGURE 2: *Voting Participation, 1963–1980*

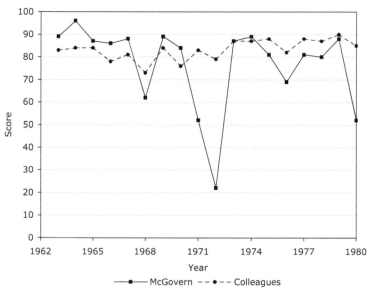

Source: *CQ Almanac,* 1963–1980

(1968, 1971, 1972, 1980). Clearly, McGovern's presidential ambitions affected his Senate activity, as his participation was substantially lower during the years he campaigned for national office. Except for Mundt, who was debilitated by a stroke in 1969 and therefore absent from the Senate, McGovern possessed the lowest voting participation rate of any senator in 1972. He voted in only 22 percent of all recorded votes that year. Similarly, he voted barely half of the time in 1971; only Mundt and one other senator had lower participation rates than McGovern in that year. Later in his career, again because of his many duties, causes, and travels beyond his Senate service, McGovern's participation fell below the rate of other Senate Democrats.

How did McGovern position himself in relation to the rest of his party? Two *CQ* measures are particularly useful in answering this question. *CQ* reports "party unity" votes—votes on bills where a majority of one party opposes a majority of the other party. For each member, *CQ* reports the percentage of times the member votes with his or her party. Figure 3 shows party-unity scores for McGovern and other Democrats from his chamber (i.e., House Democrats from 1957 to 1960 and Senate Democrats from 1963 to 1980). In general, it can be noted that party unity was stable, except for a decline around 1968. A characteristic of these data is that missed votes lower party unity and other scores. Thus, McGovern's lower voting-participation rates during his presidential campaigns (1968, 1971–1972) depreciate his party-unity scores in those years. In general, McGovern voted with other Democrats on party-line votes at higher rates than his colleagues. In fact, early in his career, he was often among the highest-rated Democrats on party-unity scores.

However, did McGovern follow the contemporary Senate norm of collegiality with members of the other party?[21] *CQ* also analyzes recorded votes on bipartisanship, that is, when majorities of both parties agree on a particular bill. Figure 4 plots these bipartisanship scores for both McGovern and his chamber's Democrats. Again, one sees the relative stability of this measure with a marked decline around 1968. For most of his congressional service, McGovern's bipartisanship scores are remarkably similar to those of his colleagues. As discussed above, McGovern's absence during his presidential campaigns of 1968 and 1971–1972 lower his bipartisanship score as compared to other Senate Democrats.

Finally, did McGovern support presidential priorities during his congressional career? CQ analyzes all messages, speeches, and public statements by each president to determine his views on pending legislation. Figure 5 graphs presidential support, or the percentage of recorded votes on which a president has taken a clear position and members have voted with the president's position. House Democratic support for President Eisenhower declined in his last term, and, in general, McGovern's votes tracked his colleagues' level of support.

During President Kennedy's last year in office and the early years of the Johnson presidency, Senate Democrats usually supported the administration's position on bills. From 1963 to 1966, McGovern was more supportive of the administration's legislation than his colleagues were. However, as antiwar protests increased in 1968, Senate Democrats, including McGovern, withdrew their support for many of Johnson's legislative bills, especially on foreign affairs. The administrations of Richard Nixon and Gerald Ford were also unsuccessful in garnering many votes from Senate Democrats. Moreover, McGovern's presidential-support scores were much lower than his colleagues' scores during these latter Republican presidencies. Both McGovern and his colleagues tended to agree with Nixon's foreign policies more than his domestic proposals. Finally, Senate Democrats, including McGovern, generally cooperated with President Jimmy Carter's legislative priorities.

In short, McGovern's voting patterns track closely with his chamber's Democrats. Throughout his congressional career, he was a more loyal Democrat than most of his colleagues; his bipartisanship scores were similar to those of other Senate Democrats. McGovern's votes do not cast him as out of step with his chamber colleagues on support for presidential proposals. Of course, the data also show that McGovern was largely inactive on the Senate floor during his presidential campaigns.

FIGURE 3: *Party Unity Scores, 1957–1980*

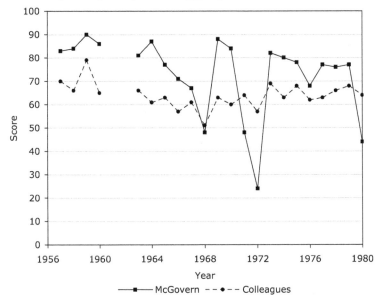

Source: *CQ Almanac*, 1957–1980

FIGURE 4: *Bipartisanship Scores, 1957–1977*

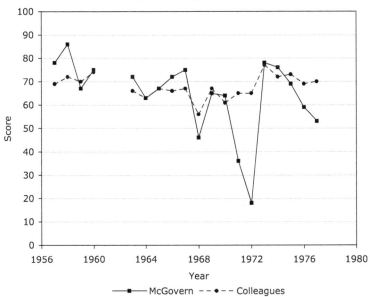

Source: *CQ Almanac*, 1957–1977

FIGURE 5: *Presidential Support, 1957–1980*

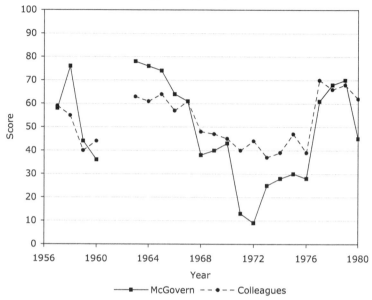

Source: *CQ Almanac*, 1957–1980

An Evaluation

Congressional careers can be judged by a number of yard-
sticks. Most members are assessed by the extent to which they
bring "pork barrel" projects home to their districts. Others receive
high marks for passing significant landmark legislation (e.g., Pell
Grants or the Wagner Act). In choosing their role in Congress,
individual members select from a wide array of styles.[22] For example, some observers may question Senate leader Robert Dole's
effectiveness because no legislation carries his name. However,
Dole was a legislative genius at finding common ground between
opponents. On countless occasions, Dole served as a mediator,
dragging legislation across the Senate floor in the closing days of
a session.

In some ways, McGovern's congressional career might appear unremarkable because he failed to get major legislation
passed. On a far grander scale, however, McGovern successfully
used his congressional experiences to articulate a vital alterna-

tive vision for the country on a number of leading issues of the day. Equally important, McGovern successfully made his arguments and forwarded his vision in terms ordinary citizens could grasp. His plain-speaking style, combined with the power of his ideas, fundamentally changed the debate in American politics. An award-winning debater, McGovern presented his arguments in a cool, rational, precise arrangement of facts and conclusions. He staked out policy positions based on a coherent, ethical framework. Simply put, he argued that unfettered militarism was a threat to world peace. In McGovern's vision, the United States should steer its resources away from war and toward stable growth and a secure social infrastructure.

NOTES

1. Robert Sam Anson, *McGovern: A Biography* (New York: Holt, Rinehart & Winston, 1972), pp. 129–32.

2. Alan L. Clem, *Government by the People?: South Dakota Politics in the Last Third of the Twentieth Century* (Rapid City, S.Dak.: Chiesman Foundation for Democracy, 2002), p. 13; Alan L. Clem, *Prairie State Politics: Popular Democracy in South Dakota* (Washington, D.C.: Public Affairs Press, 1967), pp. 38–43, 55. For more on Adlai Stevenson's role, *see* Kent M. Beck, "What Was Liberalism in the 1950s?," *Political Science Quarterly* 102 (Summer 1987): 233–58.

3. Anson, *McGovern*, pp. 68–85; George McGovern, *Grassroots: The Autobiography of George McGovern* (New York: Random House, 1977), pp. 66–71. *See* Chapter 3 by Valerie R. O'Regan and Stephen J. Stambough for a further discussion of the topic.

4. Anson, *McGovern*, pp. 75–85.

5. Ibid., pp. 87–90; Jon K. Lauck, "George S. McGovern and the Farmer: South Dakota Politics, 1953–1962," *South Dakota History* 32 (Winter 2002): 337–46.

6. Gary Aguiar, "Johnson Beats Thune in South Dakota's Senate Race," in *The Roads to Congress, 2002*, ed. Sunil Ahuja and Robert Dewhirst (n.p.: By the Editors, 2003), pp. 137–54; Clem, *Prairie State Politics*, pp. 119–20; David W. Rohde, "Risk-Bearing and Progressive Ambition: The Case of Members of the United States House of Representatives,"

American Journal of Political Science 23 (Feb. 1979): 1–26; McGovern, *Grassroots*, pp. 80–83. *See* Chapter 5 by Ahrar Ahmad for a discussion of McGovern's work with Food for Peace.

7. Anson, *McGovern*, pp. 121–28; McGovern, *Grassroots*, pp. 89–91.

8. Thomas J. Knock, "'Come Home, America': The Story of George McGovern," in *Vietnam and the American Political Tradition: The Politics of Dissent*, ed. Randall B. Woods (Cambridge, U.K.: Cambridge University Press, 2003), pp. 108–9; Anson, *McGovern*, pp. 192, 202–3, 211–14.

9. Alan I. Abramowitz, "Explaining Senate Election Outcomes," *American Political Science Review* 82 (June 1988): 388–89, 393; Anson, *McGovern*, pp. 212–17; Clem, *Government by the People*, pp. 63–64.

10. Robert L. Peabody, Norman J. Ornstein, and David W. Rohde, "The United States Senate as a Presidential Incubator: Many Are Called but Few Are Chosen," *Political Science Quarterly* 91 (Summer 1976): 237–58; Paul R. Abramson, John H. Aldrich, and David W. Rohde, "Progressive Ambition among United States Senators: 1972–1988," *Journal of Politics* 49 (1987): 3–35; Anson, *McGovern*, pp. 264–65; McGovern, *Grassroots*, pp. 159–63; Knock, "'Come Home, America': The Story of George McGovern," p. 117. *See also* Chapter 7 by John D. Schaff for a further discussion of the 1972 presidential race.

11. McGovern, *Grassroots*, pp. 257–58; Clem, *Government by the People*, p. 69.

12. Clem, *Government by the People*, p. 75.

13. Quoted ibid., p. 76.

14. Clem, *Prairie State Politics*, p. 129; Warren E. Miller and Donald E. Stokes, "Constituency Influence in Congress," *American Political Science Review* 57 (1963): 45–56.

15. Anson, *McGovern*, pp. 223–24.

16. Ibid., pp. 219–39; Knock, "'Come Home, America': The Story of George McGovern," pp. 94–95.

17. Anson, *McGovern*, pp. 130–31, 149–55; Knock, "'Come Home, America': The Story of George McGovern," pp. 100–105.

18. Anson, *McGovern*, pp. 157–60, 175–78; McGovern, *Grassroots*, pp. 164–68; Knock, "'Come Home, America': The Story of George McGovern," pp. 111–17.

19. Anson, *McGovern*, pp. 169–75, 185; McGovern, *Grassroots*, pp. 268–69.

20. Keith T. Poole and Steven R. Daniels, "Ideology, Party, and Voting in the U. S. Congress, 1959–1980," *American Political Science Review* 79 (1985): 373–99; Alan L. Clem, "Variations in Voting Blocs across Policy

Fields: Pair Agreement Scores in the 1967 U. S. Senate," *Western Political Quarterly* 23 (1970): 541–43, 547.

21. Donald R. Matthews, "The Folkways of the United States Senate: Conformity to Group Norms and Legislative Effectiveness," *American Political Science Review*, 53 (1959): 1069–73.

22. For a discussion of styles, *see* Richard Fenno, Jr., *Home Style: House Members in Their Districts* (Boston: Little, Brown & Co., 1978).

CHAPTER FIVE

GEORGE MCGOVERN AND

FOOD FOR PEACE

CONTEXT AND CONSEQUENCE

AHRAR AHMAD

*Food is strength, and food is peace, and food is freedom,
and food is a helping hand to people around the world
whose goodwill and friendship we want.*[1]
—*John F. Kennedy,
Mitchell Corn Palace, May 1960*

The International Monetary Fund (a rather conservative institution) in its special issue of *Finance and Development* in 2000 pointed out: "Of the world's 6 billion people, about 2.8 billion, almost half, live on less than $2 per day and 1.2 billion live on less than $1 a day. In the poorest countries, as many as one in every five children does not reach his or her fifth birthday and as many as half of the children under 5 are malnourished."[2] While substantial progress has been made in several areas, and in spite of the heroic efforts of many people and institutions, the condition of the majority of the world's population remains grim. It is sobering to realize that while the agricultural subsidies given to dairy farmers in Europe in 2002 amounted to approximately $2.50 per day per cow, about 75 percent of the population of Africa lives on less than that.[3]

While the decade of the 1990s witnessed a period of remarkable economic buoyancy for most of the developed countries (particularly the United States), economic progress in the developing world was meager and uneven. It is true that the number of people in the world living on less than one dollar a day has declined from 30 to 23 percent in that period, and the total number of undernourished people has decreased by about 20 million. But that is largely accounted for through advances in China and, to a lesser extent, in a few other select countries (Indonesia, Thailand, Nigeria, Ghana, and Peru). If these countries are set aside, the number of under-nourished people in the rest of the world has actually increased by about 80 million in that period; and in Africa, a deadly com-bination of food scarcities, diseases such as HIV-AIDS, internal conflicts, failed economic policies, and an unhelpful international environment have led to desperate, indeed tragic, consequences.

At the beginning of the twenty-first century, about 840 mil-lion people continue to live under conditions of chronic malnutri-tion, and approximately 24,000 people continue to die of hunger-related conditions every day. Between 50 and 60 percent of all childhood deaths in the less developed countries, including deaths caused by the four dreaded killers (diarrhea, acute respiratory ill-ness, malaria, and measles), are related to the stunting and debili-tation caused by hunger and malnutrition.[4] It is also obvious that, while poverty causes hunger, hunger also causes poverty in the sense that it impairs physical and mental growth, cripples the ca-pacity to learn and earn, and traps people into a vicious cycle from which it is difficult to escape. Fifty-four countries are compara-tively poorer today than they were in 1990, and twenty-one coun-tries have fallen behind in the Human Development Index (which consists of an integrated measure of income, life expectancy, and literacy) designed by the United Nations.[5]

In the meantime, the disparity between the more affluent and the more vulnerable countries has been exacerbated, and the gen-erosity of the richer countries (suffering from what has been called "compassion fatigue" and distracted by other pressing issues) has become less robust. The richest 1 percent of the world's popula-tion now receives as much income as the total of the poorest 57 percent, and the average income in the richest twenty countries is thirty-seven times greater than in the poorest twenty countries — a gap that has doubled in the last forty years. While the economic performance of many of the poor countries has continued to be sluggish, and at times became negative in the 1990s, the Official Development Assistance (ODA) from the Organization for Eco-nomic Cooperation and Development (OECD) countries to the

Third World has declined from .33 percent of their GNP to .24 percent between 1990 and 1999. United States aid has declined from 0.2 percent of its GNP to 0.1 percent in that period.[6] As a share of ODA, food aid has decreased from 20 percent in 1972, to 12 percent in 1981, to 6 percent in 1990.[7]

These developments are particularly ironic in the context of the fact that the amount of food grown in the world has increased at an impressive rate. Total cereal production has risen from 1.1 billion tons in 1969–1971 to 1.75 billion tons in 1988–1990, and it is expected to reach 2.35 billion tons by 2010. Obviously, the world's population has also increased during that time. However, it is apparent that the rate of increase of total food production (2.2 percent per annum between 1969 and 1999) is much higher than the rate of increase in the world's population (1.6 percent in the same period). Even in the developing countries, where the world's hungry are concentrated, population growth has been 1.9 percent per annum while agricultural production has increased by 3.5 percent. For example, per-capita food supplies have increased from 2,430 calories per day in 1969–1971 to 2,700 calories per day in 1988–1990 and are expected to go up to 2,860 calories per day by 2010. Fish production in the world has doubled from 65 million tons in 1970 to 125 million tons in 1999.[8] The problem of hunger in the world is not, nor has it ever been, an issue of the availability of food but merely of the distribution. As George McGovern asks so pointedly: "[We] have the resources and the knowledge to end hunger everywhere. The big question is, Do we have the political leadership and the will to end this scourge in our time?"[9]

George McGovern has been struggling with this question for a long time. In his autobiography, he tells us of the anguish and anxiety he felt when, as a child, he saw a grown man, a hardworking farmer, begin to cry because he could not feed his family.[10] In the 1950s, McGovern was a powerful voice in the House, along with Hubert Humphrey in the Senate, attempting to do something concrete to resolve the paradox of hunger amidst plenty, both at home and abroad. And, as director of the Food for Peace Program in 1961, he boldly and imaginatively faced the challenges and opportunities of the period. In the process, he helped to feed millions of people.

A History of Hunger Relief

The Food for Peace Program was the result of a fortuitous combination of three developments that came together during the Kennedy Administration. First, a fairly long, if spasmodic, history of American largesse towards the less fortunate of the world began to be institutionally formalized during the 1950s because of political and agricultural compulsions. Second, a gradual evolution of international conditions and humanitarian thinking crystallized in a distinctive direction at that same time. Finally, George McGovern emerged as the administrator of a program in which his vision and passion helped to blend the first two forces into a coherent pattern.

Americans are a generous people. In spite of the limitations imposed by its isolationist cocoon in the first one hundred fifty years of its existence, the United States has found ways to help people in distress. Private voluntary agencies raised almost $1 million in humanitarian assistance during the Irish famine. The food scarcities in India in 1899 similarly prompted church missions to send 165,000 bushels of corn, and the "Committee of 100" collected another $1 million for relief efforts from over twelve hundred churches in the United States. American charities were able to mobilize about $7.5 million for famine relief in China in 1920, with some remarkable private donations, e.g., $500,000 from the Rockefellers and money from special shows on Broadway. During the second crisis in 1928–1929, the United States Relief Committee for China collected another $530,000. The severe food scarcities in Russia during the early 1920s and a poignant appeal from Maxim Gorky inspired a humanitarian effort through the American Relief Administration, which disbursed about $80 million in aid (about one-fourth of it as grain supplied from the United States government storage) that helped to feed around 14 million people in Russia at the time. Voluntary agencies donated about $12 million in aid during the Bengal famine in India in 1943, and the United States Office of the Foreign War Relief provided another $9 million.[11]

But the United States Congress had always remained a bit hesitant about such efforts. While it passed the Act for the Relief of the Citizens of Venezuela in 1812, authorizing the president to purchase goods worth about fifty-thousand dollars for the purpose, and similar appropriation bills, it also turned others down with the argument that the United States Constitution did not invest Congress with the power to use public funds for foreign relief. Humanitarian efforts at the official level sometimes circumvented Congress, either through labeling donations as agricultural surplus designed to develop new markets (as the Department of Agriculture began to do, sporadically, starting in 1896) or by assuming that the donations could be claimed as presidential prerogatives (e.g., aid to earthquake victims in Sicily in 1908).[12]

The enormity of the tragedy of the First World War created new conditions and opportunities. A total of about 28 million tons of agricultural products was distributed to different countries between 1914 and 1918. Another 6.2 million tons of food were provided to European countries through relief credits voted by Congress immediately after the war. When the period of special credits ended in 1926, efforts to create a more permanent instrument through which agricultural surpluses could be distributed as humanitarian assistance proved futile. Eventually, the trauma of the Great Depression, Franklin D. Roosevelt's charismatic presence, and the foresight of his agricultural secretary Henry Wallace combined to bring about the Agricultural Adjustment Act of 1933, which not only initiated agricultural price supports and production controls but also created the mechanism through which government subsidies for agricultural exports became possible.[13]

The creation of the Commodity Credit Corporation (CCC) in 1933 with authority over the buying and selling of agricultural commodities, the slight extension of its jurisdiction by Public Law 74-320 in 1935, and the Lend-Lease Act of 1941 facilitated the shipment of agricultural products worth about $6 billion to the Allied countries during the Second World War. Further amendments to the Agricultural Adjustment Act in 1949 helped to extend the CCC's jurisdiction to sell, barter, or donate agricultural commodities. Consequently, some legislative support and bureaucratic experience in disbursing large quantities of agricultural assistance to other countries was already in place to help facilitate the launching of the Marshall Plan to assist a devastated and famished Europe after the war. Agricultural products consisting of food, feed, and fertilizer provided more than a quarter of the $13.5 billion of aid distributed through this channel between 1949 and 1951.[14] The winding down of the Marshall Plan coincided with the beginning of the Korean Conflict, which helped to absorb some of the surpluses that American farmers easily and inevitably produced.

Arrangements for surpluses that depended upon such extraordinary external circumstances were inherently unstable, however, and the need for a more reliable and appropriate policy framework relating to agriculture in general, and surplus disposal in particular, became necessary and unavoidable in the 1950s. Several considerations drove the discussion of agricultural policy. First, technological breakthroughs and new farming resources and techniques had led to an unprecedented level of productivity for American farmers. Value of total farm production increased from $10.6 billion in 1940, to $32.8 billion in 1950, and $37.4 billion in 1952. With 1967 serving as a base-year measurement of 100, the index of farm output per man-hour (for food grains) increased from 21 in 1940, to 40 in 1950, to 93 in 1960. Surplus wheat stocks rose from 13 million tons in 1952–1953 to 42 million tons by the end of 1953–1954, and the value of government-owned stocks passed the $5 billion mark by the middle of 1953.[15]

Second, many farm organizations such as the American Farm Bureau Federation, the Grange, and the National Farmers Union had become politically and organizationally more prominent. While economic and demographic shifts indicated a lessening of the farm population, 13 percent of the United States population continued to live on farms in 1952, 29 percent had been reared on farms, and a significant number depended upon agricultural production in some form or another for employment. Moreover, farmers' disproportionate presence in some crucial states, and the emotional and symbolic power they had always exerted, ensured the significance of their voices in any national debate of concern to them. The continuation of price supports, the exploration of new international markets, and the disposal of the surpluses they were producing were the issues uppermost in their minds.[16]

Finally, there had been a radical transformation in the international scene: Winston Churchill's famous "iron curtain" speech, delivered in Fulton, Missouri, in 1947; United States perceptions of Soviet economic threats in Iran, territorial threats in Turkey, and political threats in Greece; and Soviet unwillingness or inability to keep some of their promises in Eastern Europe—all these factors contributed to President Harry Truman's policy of "containment" in 1947. The world was divided along clear and aggressively drawn ideological battle lines. Not only had America emerged from its self-conscious aloofness in the world, it had become the unquestioned leader of the Free World, enthusiastically committed to combating the "evils" of Communist aggression and Soviet expansionism. It became apparent that the economic prosperity of the United States, particularly the bounty of America's agriculture, could play a vital role in that struggle, especially in weak, impoverished, newly created states coming into existence after centuries of colonial rule. In debates about agricultural policy on the floor of the House in 1954, Fred Marshall pointed out that food "can be used as a weapon. . . . in this fight against the insidious effects of communism." Brooks Hays suggested that the agricultural surpluses "can be made a far more potential means of combatting [sic] the spread of communism than the hydrogen bomb." And E. C. Gathings expressed the need to counteract the Communist propaganda that "we are permitting our food to lay up here in storehouses and rot before giving it to needy and hungry people throughout the world."[17]

PL 480 and the FAO

It was in this context, and in spite of misgivings from some members of the Eisenhower Administration, that Congress passed the Agricultural Trade Development and Assistance Act, popularly known as Public Law 480, in June 1954; the president promptly signed it. This momentous and complicated piece of legislation has gone through several amendments since its origin, but it provided the essential framework governing the relationship between domestic agricultural production and external needs and interests. The legislation was divided into three categories. Title I consisted of sales of food to "friendly" nations in foreign currencies that the United States could then use for different purposes (e.g., economic development of the recipient country, United States agricultural market development, payment of United States obligations). Title II donations were mostly intended as grants for emergencies, famine, and relief purposes and included the possibility of use in food-for-work projects. The "friendliness" of the government was not a criterion. Title III enabled the distribution of food to private voluntary organizations that could use it for school-lunch and disaster-relief programs at home or for other humanitarian purposes abroad. The president could also exchange food for strategic materials and commodities not produced in the United States.

Initially, the PL 480 program appeared successful. Shipments of agricultural products in the first full year of the act's operation in 1955 totaled 3.4 million tons valued at $384,000, but in two years, shipments reached 14 million tons valued at $1.5 billion.[18] Writing in 1964, McGovern pointed out that approximately 120 million tons of food valued at $13 billion ("enough to fill three large ships each day for ten years") had left American harbors, representing 27 percent of all United States agricultural exports and about two-thirds of wheat exports during that ten-year period.[19] However, as helpful as this dispersal of goods was to the American economy, particularly to the American farmer, several problems began to emerge.

First, the hybrid nature of PL 480 and its multiple objectives (surplus disposal, market development, foreign policy, humanitarian relief, and economic development) meant that it would have to serve many and diverse constituencies (farmers, exporters, military, diplomats, charitable groups, development professionals, and so on). While this situation provided flexibility, it also made the food program vulnerable to shifting priorities and interests and provoked fierce interagency wrangling. The Agriculture, Commerce, State, Defense, and Treasury Departments all engaged in both protective and predatory jostling.[20] McGovern noted that the program was "burdened with interagency delay, bureaucratic timidity and Executive branch fears of Congressional reaction."[21]

Second, and more importantly, there was the general sense that while some good was being achieved, more could be accomplished. Several studies were conducted, the most far-reaching being Hubert Humphrey's report titled *Food and Fiber as a Force for Freedom*, which he presented to the Senate Committee on Agriculture in 1958. The report pointed out that some countries accepted PL 480 commodities as a favor to the United States; that the act led to the perception that the United States was "dumping" its excess on the world; that the program was hampered by its ad hoc character, depending upon yearly appropriations; and that the administrative structure of the program was inadequate and indifferent to its essential purposes. The most stinging criticism charged that the program was conducted for narrow, utilitarian, and commercial goals of "surplus disposal" rather than fulfilling its larger, nobler, more humanitarian impulses. Humphrey argued that the surpluses could be used as a constructive force for human development, promoting "welfare, peace, and freedom on a world scale." In 1959, the phrase "food for peace" became part of the bill (S.1711) that Humphrey introduced in the Senate to overhaul the mechanics and priorities of PL 480.[22]

George McGovern expressed similar sentiments in the House with equal passion and eloquence. Long a foe of the phrase "surplus disposal," which he thought was "an insult to hungry people," he wholeheartedly supported Humphrey's language and efforts. He also pointed out the high cost of food storage, approaching $1 billion in 1958. He thundered in House debates, "Can the President not see that, rather than a 'burden' to be deplored, agricultural abundance is one of America's greatest assets for raising living standards and promoting peace and stability in the free world?"[23]

The international situation had also changed toward the end of the Eisenhower period. First, the Cold War took on new meaning and dimensions. In China, Maoist rhetoric and mobilizing capabilities bolstered old concerns about the "yellow peril." Similarly, the Cuban revolution surprised most Americans. The U2 spy plane brought down in the Soviet Union proved to be deeply embarrassing, and most ominously, the conflict in Indochina was increasingly seducing the United States into its morally chaotic and militarily uncertain vortex.

Second, the extent of human misery and desperation in the world began to be more evident. The situation was clearly demonstrated in two countries that claimed the attention of the United States for moral or political reasons. There was India, land of mysticism and Gandhi, the most populous democracy in the world. And there was Pakistan, less prone to democracy but more amenable to American anti-Communist motivations, serving, for example, as an ally in building a security cordon around Soviet interests and ambitions in the region. Both countries suffered from massive structural underdevelopment with much of their population living in grinding, brutalizing, dehumanizing poverty. At the same time, the process of gradual decolonization of Africa was generating a crisis of rising expectations. Many Africans who had hoped for development and prosperity after independence were now faced with increasing levels of despair and deprivation. The reality of such suffering could not be ignored indefinitely.

Compounding the problems was the clear potential for a veritable population explosion in many of these countries. World population increased from 2.5 billion in 1950 to 3.04 billion in 1960 and reached 3.7 billion a few years thereafter, with annual growth rates that increased from .61 percent in 1920, to 1.47 percent in 1950, and, for the first time in human history, more than 2 percent in 1970. By that time, 78 million people increased the world's population annually. In 1920, the world's population had been expected to double in 113 years; in 1950, it was 47 years; in 1970, 33 years. The extrapolations in the 1950s were even scarier, and the apocalyptic vision of Thomas Malthus, who predicted mass starvation as food production failed to keep pace with human reproduction, was repeatedly invoked. The vast majority of the burgeoning population lived in the underdeveloped areas of the world.[24]

Third, the international attitude regarding the inequities of the world, particularly the plight of its hungry millions, was gradually changing. In this respect, the role of the United Nations and its associate agencies was becoming increasingly noteworthy. Some humanitarian organizations founded under the auspices of the UN and charged with multilateral food distribution languished (e.g., the United Nations Relief and Rehabilitation Association from which the United States effectively withdrew in 1947), but others began to acquire greater political relevance and moral authority. One of the most important was the Food and Agricul-

ture Organization (FAO), which owed its origin to a meeting convened by President Franklin D. Roosevelt at Hot Springs, Virginia,
in 1943. The forty-four participating governments had agreed, in
principle, to a permanent institution to deal with issues relevant to
hunger and food. The FAO was formally organized in 1945 after all
the member nations endorsed a constitution drawn up by Lester
Pearson of Canada. The first director general of FAO, John Boyd-
Orr, was enthusiastic about an active and interventionist organization that focused mainly on humanitarian concerns. "Food is
more than a trade commodity," he argued. "It is an essential of
life."[25]

In 1946, Boyd-Orr advocated the formation of a world food
board that would enjoy broad authority to stabilize the price of
agricultural goods, establish a food reserve for any emergencies,
provide funds for disposal of surplus food, and coordinate credit,
trade, and commodity policy to help alleviate the problems of food
insecurity in the world. The plan, considered excessively broad by
industrialized countries like the United States and incomplete in
terms of logistical details, was rejected at the time.[26] However,
such idealism became the ideological subtext infusing the FAO
in the early years. Pioneering empirical research, patient advocacy, and successive studies, proposals, and conferences helped to
create the intellectual basis "for an operational multilateral food
aid agency to play a key role in changing surpluses from burden
to asset by their use in support of projects and programmes to
achieve development."[27] The FAO "Freedom from Hunger Campaign" reached its high point in 1960 when the UN General Assembly overwhelmingly adopted Resolution 1496, "The Provision
of Food Surpluses to Food Deficit Peoples through the United
Nations System," and authorized the director general of FAO to
undertake a study to determine its mechanics and dynamics.[28]

The United States not only supported the resolution but, in
fact, was instrumental in introducing it. This advocacy signified a
major shift in United States policy towards multilateral food aid.
Responding to political pressures at home and abroad, the Eisenhower Administration made a practical adjustment to the realities
it was compelled to face. The McGovern and Humphrey proposals
for PL 480 in 1959 and the need to out-flank the Kennedy cam-

paign in 1960 gave impetus to the administration's efforts. Growing surpluses that needed disposal, particularly after the European Economic Community's Common Agricultural Policy in
1958 that limited United States food sales to Europe, also spurred
Eisenhower's sponsorship of the UN resolution.[29] However, it was
John F. Kennedy's victory in the 1960 elections and his appointment of George McGovern to head the Food for Peace Program
that brought about decisive change in United States leadership.

Ambassador for World Hunger

McGovern's background had prepared him well for the challenges he would face as an advocate for eradicating world hunger. His father had exemplified the spiritual and social commit-
ments of a gentle Methodist minister who had been moved by
the suffering of the people during the Great Depression. A man
who would occasionally bring home a hungry guest, he sensi-
tized his children to the plight of the more vulnerable segments
of society. In fact, in the 1940s, George McGovern had enrolled in
a seminary and was preparing to follow in his father's footsteps.
The younger McGovern's populist inspirations, sense of community, and a natural dedication to fairness were also derived from
his midwestern rural roots. His experience in the military during WWII earned him the Distinguished Flying Cross for valor
and provided him with his fierce patriotism as well as his pronounced ambivalence about military solutions to human problems. His education at Dakota Wesleyan University and Northwestern University exposed him to several iconoclastic and activist
scholars and awakened in him a more internationalist and critical understanding of the processes of historical change. He ac-
quired a healthy skepticism about Cold War paranoia and a deeper
appreciation of the complex relationship between political power
and social justice.[30] Through it all, he developed a rugged independence of intellect and judgment, an uncompromising moral
dignity, an enduring compassion for the less fortunate, and a rhe-
torical boldness that allowed him, against all odds, to win a seat
in the United States House of Representatives in 1956. True to his
origin and interests, McGovern's first speech on the floor of the
House was a critique of Eisenhower's agricultural policies.[31]

In 1960, McGovern failed in his bid for a Senate seat, losing to Karl Mundt by only 1 percent of votes cast. During the campaign, he and John F. Kennedy stumped together in South Dakota. In Congress, they had respected each other and cooperated on labor-related legislation. Now Kennedy, who had never been enthusiastic about agricultural issues, listened to McGovern's ideas, which were reflected, to some extent, in Kennedy's Corn Palace speech in Mitchell, South Dakota, where he spoke of food as peace and freedom. The extent of Kennedy's contribution to McGovern's defeat may never be known, but Kennedy himself believed that he had cost McGovern the election. After his campaign appearance in South Dakota, Kennedy confided to his brother Robert, "I think we just cost that nice guy a Senate seat."[32]

It was widely speculated that McGovern, because of his experience, expertise, interests, and loyalty to the Kennedys, would be rewarded with the post of secretary of agriculture in the new administration. He did not get that position but received an offer that was probably much richer in appeal and prospect. In his third day in office and through his second executive order, President Kennedy created the Office of Food for Peace, thus appropriating the language preferred by Humphrey and McGovern. The president located the new program in the Executive Office in the White House, thereby shielding it from the bureaucratic tangles it would otherwise face. Kennedy named McGovern as its director, giving him the title of Special Assistant to the President and elevating the rank of his office to that of undersecretary (or "virtual Cabinet-level," as Kennedy put it), thus indicating the importance of the program and the president's personal commitment to it.[33]

McGovern's earnestness and Kennedy's support were soon evident. In his first State of the Union Address, Kennedy announced that McGovern would undertake the first foreign mission of his administration by going to Brazil and Argentina to witness and report on local conditions and needs. The trip, taken with Arthur Schlesinger, moved McGovern. He came back and immediately undertook to send to Brazil 16,000 tons of corn and beans and enough dried milk to feed 2 million people for a year. The United States should react in this way, he told Kennedy, "not for economic or political reasons, but because it was the morally proper thing

President John F. Kennedy created the special office of Food for Peace, appointing McGovern as director.

to do."[34] In six months, Food for Peace sent about 264,173 tons of food to several countries; that represented more than six times the total amount of food delivered under Title II of PL 480 during the entire Eisenhower Administration.[35]

McGovern also helped to establish the Food for Wages Program through which people in less-developed countries would be encouraged to undertake public works projects and be remunerated with American agricultural products. "By October 1963, twenty-two countries were participating in Food for Wages," McGovern records, "and the flow of Food for Peace development aid had reached almost a million tons."[36] About seven hundred thousand people in these countries were partially paid from this initiative for working on projects such as building roads, hospitals, schools, agricultural development, and reforestation. But McGovern's pet project was the school-lunch program that helped to improve health, educational retention, and life opportunities for the children of the less-developed countries. Thanks to his determination, 35 million children in Latin America, Asia, and Africa began receiving a daily lunch at school by 1962, and two years later, over 1 million children in Peru, 2 million in South Korea, 3.5 million in Egypt, 4.5 million in Brazil, 9 million in India, and over 10 million in Southeast Asia were also benefitting from this program.[37] These results led historian Thomas Knock to conclude, "The Peace Corps not excepted, McGovern had superintended the single greatest humanitarian achievement of the Kennedy-Johnson era."[38]

Most of these efforts signified unilateral transfers of American resources to other countries, but McGovern's involvement with Food for Peace was probably more notable for another accomplishment that was as dramatic in its impact as it was unconventional in the way it came about. Pursuant to the United Nations resolution in 1960 regarding the channeling of food surpluses to needy countries, the FAO had undertaken a study of how to implement the resolution and its Intergovernmental Advisory Committee met in Rome in April 1961 to discuss the recommendations. Kennedy requested McGovern to represent the United States at this meeting. McGovern's attitude had already been indicated in a report he had sent to the president in March 1961, suggesting that the United

In February 1962, Senator McGovern visited this classroom in Cairo, Egypt, to observe the school-lunch program in action. These children were drinking from sterilized glass bottles rather than the usual tin cups.

States Food for Peace agenda and a multilateral food-distribution program were not mutually exclusive because "world food needs are so great that there is need for both approaches."[39]

On the way to Rome, McGovern requested his staff (particularly Ray Ioanes from the Department of Agriculture and Sidney Jacques from the State Department) to draft a proposal for a multilateral food-distribution system. This idea had not been discussed, let alone cleared, with the president or any relevant authorities, nor was it consistent with the proposed format or objectives of the meeting. McGovern nonetheless persisted, received the appropriate permission from the White House over the weekend through telephone contacts, and presented his brief nine-point plan on Monday in Rome. McGovern committed the United States to supporting multilateral food-aid programs, promised $40 million in commodity and $10 million in cash contributions towards a proposed total of $100 million, and outlined a three-year experimental trial for the program. Almost single-handedly, through a combination of courage, confidence, and charm, he set in motion the process and the inspiration that would evolve into the World Food Programme (WFP), which came into existence in 1963.[40]

The WFP has emerged as a critical component in the struggle against hunger and inequality in the world. At the end of its three-year experimental period in 1965, total resources committed to WFP reached $93.7 million; 32 emergency operations had been carried out in 25 countries; and 116 development projects were supported. In 1965 alone, 200,000 workers were employed by WFP projects, and about 1 million people benefited from its programs. Between 1963 and 2001, the WFP invested about $24 billion and distributed more than 43 million tons of food to combat hunger, provide emergency relief, and promote social and economic development in the less-developed countries of the world. In 2002 alone, about 3.7 million tons of food were distributed to 72 million people in 82 countries at a cost of $1.59 billion. The WFP still bears the imprint of George McGovern's founding spirit in the titles of its various programs, such as Food for Life, which emphasizes emergency relief; Food for Growth, which concentrates on the more vulnerable segments of the population (e.g., 78 percent of beneficiaries of WFP activities in 2001 were

women and children), and Food for Work, which focuses on public projects. In its range, imagination, and effectiveness, WFP continues to be the preeminent humanitarian agency in the world.[41]

Beginning in 1963, the Food for Peace Program suffered two external "shocks." McGovern resigned in 1962 to run for, and win, a
Senate seat; Kennedy was assassinated in 1963. The program was
transferred to the State Department, where bureaucratic infight-
ing and factionalism became increasingly convoluted and debilitating as time went on. Gradual politicization of the program occurred as most resources under its jurisdiction were diverted to
Vietnam and Cambodia as accessories to war rather than instruments of peace. The soaring idealism that had characterized its
early enthusiasm was progressively depleted. Moreover, there was
a gradual perception among the American public, fed and perhaps
manipulated by some of the nation's leadership, that it was better
to be feared than loved and that the meaning of national security
in foreign-policy analysis dealt with physical conflict only. Conse-
quently, militarist imperatives began to overwhelm humanitarian
instincts as an approach to the world and its problems.[42]

Conclusion

While he may have formally resigned from the position of director of the Office of Food for Peace in 1962, McGovern himself
never abandoned the world's poor. In 1964, he wrote, "The mere
absence of warfare in a world where half the people are hungry is
not real peace. . . . A positive concept of peace includes a concerted
attack on the chronic enemies of all men, of which hunger is the
most basic."[43] In a 1965 speech to the Senate on this most important war against hunger, McGovern made references to utilitarian arguments for food aid (to combat international Communism,
protect the interests of American farmers, explore new markets,
and so on), but his primary goal remained the welfare of the
world's poor. He pledged "a people's war with corn instead of
cannon, with farmers instead of marines, with agricultural technology instead of battle plans, with food instead of fear."[44] He
introduced the International Food and Nutrition Act in 1965 that
would provide half a billion dollars for seven years (1) to purchase
agricultural commodities from United States farmers to distrib-

ute abroad and (2) to sponsor measures (including university research) to strengthen agricultural projects in less-developed countries. In 1974, at the UN Food Conference in Rome, he proposed
a reduction of 10 percent of the military budgets of the developed
countries (so that they not "waste their substance in military overkill") and a contribution of 10 percent of the windfall profits of the
OPEC countries (so that they not "accumulate riches beyond reasonable use"). These combined funds would be directed towards
the alleviation of poverty and hunger in the world.[45] In 1975, he
continued to be haunted by "those eyes, the stark, anxious eyes,
the eyes which plead without words, the eyes of the hungry children, for whom the early years will be the last years," and he never
wavered in his commitment to put his shoulder to the stone and
endure.[46]

In 1997, when President William Clinton named McGovern
to be United States ambassador to the cluster of UN food-related
agencies—the FAO, WFP, and IFAD (International Fund for Agricultural Development, which provides low-interest loans for agricultural projects)—the South Dakota native persisted in nudging
the world toward more humane and peaceful directions. Today,
McGovern's speeches and writings continue to offer the possibility and the challenge that the number of hungry people in the
world can be halved by 2015 and hunger itself be eliminated by
2030.[47] Even if we do not achieve those goals, McGovern's idealism will surely encourage the efforts. While the situation regarding hunger and poverty in the world is not particularly happy, it
would have been far worse had it not been for the compassionate
activism that he demonstrated. Food for Peace was not merely a
set of policies for George McGovern, it was a metaphor that captured his world view, defined his authentic humanity, and testified
to his infectious optimism.

I would like to end this chapter on a personal note. Growing
up in Dhaka, Bangladesh, in the early 1960s, I remember my sis-
ters bringing home cheese and dried milk from the girls' public school that they attended. I myself went to a private Catholic
institution and hence was not eligible for such government programs. I remember impishly putting fistfuls of the dried milk into
my mouth, my siblings pleading for the pudding that they craved,

and my mother looking forward to using the shiny tins for storing things after the milk and cheese were finished. There was this slight awkwardness, however, because cultural traditions dictated that acceptance of generosity must be accompanied by expressions of appropriate gratitude. Today, on behalf of my family and of millions of others, I would simply like to say, however belatedly, "Thank you, Mr. McGovern."

NOTES

I am deeply indebted to Professor Thomas Knock of Southern Methodist University for sharing his paper on Food for Peace with me. It set a standard impossible to reach and cast an intellectual shadow difficult to escape. I am also grateful to Pratap Narain, statistical officer, Food and Agriculture Organization, Rome, for sending me much relevant information; to George Earley and David Salomon, Black Hills State University, for reading the paper and offering many helpful suggestions; and to Robert Watson, editor of the book, for his patience and encouragement. The usual caveats apply.

1. Quoted in George McGovern, *Grassroots: The Autobiography of George McGovern* (New York: Random House, 1977), p. 83.

2. Quoted in Fred J. Hitzhusen, "Context, Concepts and Policy on Poverty and Inequality," in *Food, Security and Environmental Quality in the Developing World*, ed. Rattan Lal et al. (Boca Raton, Fla.: Lewis Publishers, 2003), p. 417. The same information is available in *World Development Report, 2000/2001: Attacking Poverty* (New York: Oxford University Press for the World Bank, 2001), p. 3.

3. Barry Bearak, "Why People Still Starve," *New York Times Magazine*, 13 July 2003, p. 36.

4. The statistics in this and the preceding paragraph are gleaned from the home pages of the Food and Agriculture Organization of the United Nations (www.fao.org) and the World Food Programme in Rome (www.wfp.org) and from the *State of Food Insecurity* (Rome: Food and Agriculture Organization, 2002). Specific areas of the web sites were brought to my attention by Pratap Narain of Food and Agriculture Organization (FAO), Rome, 31 July 2003.

5. Larry Elliott, "The Lost Decade," *The Guardian*, 9 July 2003. The *Human Development Report* is published annually by the United Nations Development Program.

6. Hitzhusen, "Context, Concept and Policy on Poverty and Inequality," p. 419; Theodore H. Cohn, *Global Political Economy: Theory and*

Practice, 2d ed. (New York: Longman, 2003), pp. 405, 421. It is instructive to realize that ODA from the OECD to the Third World countries has tended to decline from 1960 onwards except for 1980. OECD countries had provided .52 percent of their GNP as aid to the Third World in 1960, .34 percent in 1970, .37 percent in 1980 .33 percent in 1990, and .24 percent in 1999. The comparable figures for the United States are .53 percent, .31 percent, .27 percent, .21 percent, and .10 percent. The OECD is a grouping of thirty democratic countries, including the United States.

7. John Shaw and Edward Clay, eds., *World Food Aid: Experiences of Recipients & Donors* (Rome: World Food Programme, 1993), p. 8. *See also* the testimony of Raymond F. Hopkins in hearings before the United States Congress, where he indicates that the United States used to supply about 95 percent of the world's food aid in the 1950s when it first authorized food aid. By 1990, aid had declined to about 60 percent in tonnage and only about 50 percent of the value of food aid distributed in the world. U.S., Congress, House, Committee on Foreign Affairs, *Issues Related to the Reauthorization of Food for Peace and Agricultural Export Promotion Programs*, 101st Cong., 2d sess., 1990, pp. 111, 123. For the pattern of declining United States contributions in the 1990s, *see* U.S., Congress, House, Committee on Agriculture, *Review of Public Law 480, The Food for Peace Program*, 104th Cong., 1st sess., 1995, p. 94. *See also* Donald G. McClelland, *United States Food Aid and Sustainable Development: Forty Years of Experience*, USAID Program and Operations Assessment Report, No. 22 (n.p.: U.S. Agency for International Development, 1998), pp. 3–6.

8. Nikos Alexandratos, ed., *World Agriculture: Towards 2010, An FAO Study* (Chichester, England: Food & Agriculture Organization of the United Nations and John Wiley & Sons, 1995), pp. 84, 118; "World Agriculture: Towards 2015/2030: Summary Report," www.fao.org/docrep/004/y3557e/y3557e04.htm, accessed 8 June 2004.

9. McGovern, *The Third Freedom: Ending Hunger in Our Time* (New York: Simon & Schuster, 2001), p. 13.

10. McGovern, *Grassroots*, p. 10.

11. Robert G. Stanley, *Food for Peace: Hope and Reality of U. S. Food Aid* (New York: Gordon & Breach, 1973), pp. 9–24.

12. George McGovern, *War against Want: America's Food for Peace Program* (New York: Walker & Co., 1964), pp. 12–13; Hans Singer, John Wood, and Tony Jennings, *Food Aid: The Challenge and the Opportunity* (Oxford: Clarendon Press, 1987), p. 17.

13. Mitchel B. Wallerstein, *Food for War—Food for Peace: United States*

Food Aid in a Global Context (Cambridge, Mass.: MIT Press, 1980), p. 27;
Singer, Wood, and Jennings, *Food Aid*, pp. 18–19.

14. Wallerstein, *Food for War—Food for Peace*, p. 32; Singer, Wood,
and Jennings, *Food Aid*, p. 20. Incidentally, these two sources provide
slightly different percentages for the proportion of food, feed, and fer-
tilizer that was part of the aid package of the Marshall Plan. Wallerstein
suggests that it was 29 percent, Singer 25 percent.

15. U.S., Department of Commerce, Bureau of the Census, *Historical
Statistics of the United States: Colonial Times to 1970, Part I*, Bicentennial Ed. (Washington, D.C.: Government Printing Office, 1975), pp. 481,
500; Singer, Wood, and Jennings, *Food Aid*, p. 22; Wallerstein, *Food for
War—Food for Peace*, pp. 34–35.

16. Peter A. Toma, *The Politics of Food for Peace: Executive-Legislative
Interaction*, Institute of Government Research, American Government
Studies, No. 2 (Tucson: University of Arizona Press, 1967), pp. 1–2,
15–16.

17. U.S., Congress, House, Subcommittee on Foreign Agricultural
Policy, *Food for Peace, 1954–1978: Major Changes in Legislation*, 96th
Cong., 1st sess., 1979, p. 3.

18. Ibid., p. 4.

19. McGovern, *War against Want*, p. 21.

20. James E. Austin, *Nutrition Programs in the Third World: Cases and
Readings* (Cambridge, Mass.: Oelgeschlager, Gunn & Hain, 1981), p. 56.

21. Quoted in Toma, *Politics of Food for Peace*, p. 71. Toma is good at
dissecting organizational and procedural complexities that sometimes
hampered the effectiveness of the programs; *see*, in particular, chapters
5 and 6. It should be pointed out that food aid has not been universally
considered an unmixed blessing. Critics of food aid have focused on
definition of terms (e.g., of food, aid, and hunger); on who gets food, in
what form, and under what conditions; and on disincentive effects of
food aid (e.g., depressing prices in local markets, external influences on
development plans, disruption in internal labor structures, changing
cultural norms and food habits, creating dependency on others, etc.).
See Simon Maxwell, "The Disincentive Effect of Food Aid: A Pragmatic
Approach," in *Food Aid Reconsidered: Assessing the Impact on Third World
Countries*, ed. Edward Clay and Olav Stokke (London: Frank Cass, 1991),
pp. 66–90. It should also be pointed out, however, that properly con-
ceived and fairly administered aid strategies could address each of these
concerns.

22. Subcommittee on Foreign Agricultural Policy, *Food for Peace,
1954–1978*, pp. 4–5. *See also* Vernon W. Ruttan, "The Politics of U.S. Food

Policy: A Historical Review," in *Why Food Aid?*, ed. Ruttan (Baltimore: Johns Hopkins University Press, 1993), p. 10.

23. McGovern, *Third Freedom*, p. 49. *See also* Thomas J. Knock, "Feeding the World and Thwarting the Communists: George McGovern and Food for Peace," in *Architects of the American Century: Individuals and Institutions in Twentieth-Century U.S. Foreign Policymaking*, ed. David F. Schmitz and T. Christopher Jespersen (Chicago: Imprint Publications, 2000), pp. 101, 116n.13.

24. John R. Weeks, *Population: An Introduction to Concepts and Issues*, 8th ed. (Belmont, Calif.: Wadsworth, 2002), pp. 8–9; George McGovern, ed., *Agricultural Thought in the Twentieth Century* (Indianapolis: Bobbs-Merrill Co., 1967), pp. 520–21. For selections from the national press about the dire warnings regarding food and population in the 1950s and 60s, *see* George McGovern, ed., *Food and Population: The World in Crisis*, Great Contemporary Issues Series (New York: Arno Press for the *New York Times*, 1975). The phrase "population explosion" was itself coined in the 1950s.

25. Boyd-Orr, quoted in Patricia L. Kutzner, *World Hunger: A Reference Handbook* (Santa Barbara, Calif.: ABC-CLIO, 1991), p. 18.

26. John Cathie, *The Political Economy of Food Aid* (New York: St. Martin's Press, 1982), pp. 32–33.

27. Singer, Wood, and Jennings, *Food Aid*, p. 27.

28. Cathie, *Political Economy of Food Aid*, p. 37.

29. Wallerstein, *Food for War—Food For Peace*, p. 93.

30. McGovern, *Grassroots*, pp. 3–51. Some of the intellectual influences of McGovern's teachers, particularly his mentor Arthur Link, are described in Knock, "Feeding the World," pp. 103–4.

31. McGovern, *Grassroots*, p. 76. *See also* Jon K. Lauck, "George S. McGovern and the Farmer: South Dakota Politics, 1953–1962," *South Dakota History* 32 (Winter 2002): 341–42.

32. Quoted in McGovern, *Grassroots*, p. 83.

33. Robert Sam Anson, *McGovern: A Biography* (New York: Holt, Rinehart & Winston, 1972), pp. 100–105.

34. McGovern, *Third Freedom*, p. 55.

35. Ibid., pp. 55–56; Knock, "Feeding the World," p. 106.

36. McGovern, *Third Freedom*, p. 56.

37. Ibid., p. 56; Knock, "Feeding the World," p. 106.

38. Knock, "Feeding the World," p. 107. *See also* McGovern, *Third Freedom*, pp. 56–57.

39. McGovern, quoted in D. John Shaw, *The UN World Food Pro-*

gramme and the Development of Food Aid (Houndsmill, England: Palgrave, 2001), pp. 6–7.

40. Ibid., pp. 6–9, 18. In this definitive history of the World Food Programme, Shaw titles Chapter 2 on its inception, "The Birth of WFP: One Man's Inspiration" (pp. 6–19).

41. Shaw, *UN World Food Programme*, p. 62; World Food Programme, "About WFP: Facts and Figures," www.wfp.org/aboutwfp/facts/2002/index.html, accessed 27 June 2004. The WFP website also contains the agency's annual reports.

42. Knock, "Feeding the World," pp. 109–13. Catherine Bertini, executive director of the WFP in 1995, pointed out that many Americans suffer from the misconception that 15 to 20 percent of the federal budget is spent on foreign aid when actually it is "less than 1 percent. . . . And food aid is only one-tenth or less of that. . . . Americans give an average of $44 per year for foreign aid. Canadians give twice that much. . . . The Norwegians average over $300 apiece" (quoted in U.S., Congress, House, Committee on Agriculture, *Review of Public Law 480, The Food for Peace Program*, 104th Cong., 1st sess., 1995, pp. 9–10). While Americans continue to provide the largest absolute amount in foreign aid, as a percentage of the country's GNP it is the lowest among the OECD countries, and the ratio has been progressively declining. *See* footnote 6 above. It is intriguing to note that popular support for American military expenditure continues to be high even though America currently spends more on the military than the rest of the world combined.

43. McGovern, *War against Want*, p. 11.

44. McGovern, *Agricultural Thought in the Twentieth Century*, p. 526.

45. McGovern, *Grassroots*, p. 271.

46. McGovern, Introduction to *Food and Population*, p. vii.

47. These goals emerged from the World Food Summit held in Rome in 1996 and are the argument of McGovern's latest book, *Third Freedom*, p. 13. It is becoming increasingly obvious that the goal is not realistically attainable, but people like McGovern keep the moral imperative in sharp focus and, in not being willing to surrender, keep the hope alive.

CHAPTER SIX

GEORGE MCGOVERN AND THE PROMISE
OF A NEW DEMOCRAT

REFORM AND ELECTORAL POLITICS IN
THE DEMOCRATIC PARTY, 1968–1970

STEPHEN K. WARD

 The Democratic party had dominated American politics in both intellectual creativity and electoral success since the 1930s. In domestic politics, the party had supported the causes of labor and civil rights; in foreign affairs, it had vowed to contain international Communism on every front. Beginning in 1965, however, the party began to break apart. The escalation of the Vietnam War by the Johnson Administration divided Democrats into "hawks and doves." On the domestic front, the legislative successes of the civil-rights movement spurred momentum toward social and economic equality in the form of Johnson's Great Society. While Americans argued over the definition of patriotism, they also debated the merits of welfare and economic integration, as blacks and other disaffected minorities demanded economic equality with whites. With Richard Nixon's defeat of Hubert Humphrey in the presidential election of 1968, Democrats struggled to heal their divided party. In the aftermath of this pivotal election, the national party turned to George McGovern, who had essentially created the Democratic party in South Dakota and had a vision for revitalizing Democratic voters across the country.

Throughout 1969 and 1970, McGovern led the Commission on Party Structure and Delegate Selection established by the Democratic National Committee to reform state party procedures for selecting delegates to the national convention. By requiring each state Democratic party to send blacks, women, and youth as delegates to the national convention in numbers proportionate to their population in the state, the commission sought to mend the tear created by the war and a changing social climate. In addition, commission members developed guidelines designed to increase the number of presidential primaries and to open up party conventions to rank-and-file members, whose antiwar voices had been ignored at the 1968 Democratic National Convention in Chicago. In the end, the McGovern Commission, as it came to be known, did not restore the traditional Democratic party but served instead as a catalyst for a new brand of politics that diminished the influence of labor and local party bosses and opened the organization to new voices.[1]

In 1972, the incumbent president Richard Nixon defeated George McGovern in a landslide election. The press and political pundits alike immediately sketched a critique of the vanquished McGovern campaign that has gone almost unchallenged ever since. The morning after the election, the *New York Times*, for instance, congratulated McGovern for his "gallant" campaign and his "confidence . . . in the rightness of his vision of America." The editorial acknowledged, however, that "because his political base was too narrow . . . [and] his social outlook allegedly too radical, Mr. McGovern lost."[2] Theodore White, the preeminent chronicler of presidential campaigns of the 1960s and 1970s, echoed the interpretation, although in less empathetic terms. He concluded that while McGovern and his supporters had remained true to their beliefs, the majority of Americans found them threatening.[3]

During the 1980s, as Ronald Reagan ushered in what came to be called the Republican Revolution, critics pointed to the McGovern Commission as the root of Democratic electoral defeats. To conservative intellectuals, in particular, the McGovern Commission represented the quintessential example of meddling liberalism in America. The commission's reforms, they contended, not only contributed to election failure but also exemplified liberal attempts to micromanage American society and its institutions. Rigid rules and sterile quotas, critics argued, blocked established means of electing delegates to the national convention and kept experienced, knowledgeable Democrats out of the nominating process.[4] Among the most vocal critics was historian Ronald Radosh, an erstwhile leftist, who placed responsibility for what he described as the "decline of the Democratic Party" squarely on the shoulders of George McGovern and the reform commission he chaired. "Gearing the party to liberal constituency groups and activists rather than to the traditional Democratic electorate," Radosh observed, "McGovern [opened] up the party to a course that would over the decades result in a steady loss of electoral support."[5] Other neoconservative writers have dismissed the commission's actions as ideological folly. In so doing, they have inferred that, had the Democrats not reformed themselves, the party would have chosen a stronger candidate in 1972, perhaps defeating President Nixon and stemming the tide of conservatism that surfaced in the 1980s.[6]

The real story of the McGovern Commission, however, must be told in the context of the political climate in which it was created, not in the politics of the 1980s. Those who served on the commission and supported its work did so as a rational, and well-considered, response to the tumultuous 1968 national convention, in which antiwar protestors fought police outside the hall and antiwar delegates were kept in check by party leaders beholden to Lyndon Johnson inside the hall. After Hubert Humphrey's disheartening loss to Richard Nixon, the commission became the most dynamic entity within the party. The fervor of reform-oriented groups, the vast potential of a new generation of young voters, and the results of the midterm elections of 1970 convinced party leaders, including McGovern, of the promise of the reform path. In the reformers' view, the McGovern Commission may have saved the nation's oldest political party from impending death.

A Party in Turmoil

With the exception of the presidency of Dwight D. Eisenhower in the 1950s, the Democratic party occupied the White House—and directed the country's political agenda—from 1933 until the inauguration of Richard Nixon in 1969. By the late 1960s, however, the party was being split apart by the Vietnam War overseas and social movements at home. Gradually, influential liberals ceased to view Communism as a unified, Soviet conspiracy but rather as a more diverse, regional phenomenon. They concluded that it was no longer necessary to oppose Communists militarily on every part of the globe, particularly in Vietnam. The liberals' criticism of President Johnson's Vietnam policy spilled into the domestic sphere, as well. "We have opposed the Vietnam War not because we are preoccupied with one issue," claimed one activist group, the Americans for Democratic Action (ADA), "but because it has blighted every liberal and progressive program here at home."[7]

Some Democrats recognized the politically debilitating nature of the widening breach in the party and worked to circumvent its effects before the 1968 presidential election. In August 1967, Allard Lowenstein founded the Conference of Concerned Democrats (CCD) so that antiwar Democrats could organize a challenge to Lyndon Johnson's bid for a second term in office. In February 1968, the CCD met in Chicago to rally support for ending the Vietnam War. During his keynote address, Congressman Don Edwards observed that "the Democratic Party was in shambles after the 1966 mid-term elections," in which the party had lost forty-seven seats in the House of Representatives and eight governorships. "The cost of [the Vietnam] war is infinite," he continued. "We have to mend the division in the Democratic Party by ending this war."[8]

To this end, Eugene McCarthy and later Robert Kennedy challenged Lyndon Johnson in the 1968 presidential primaries. McCarthy's relative success in the New Hampshire primary and the entry of Kennedy into the race convinced Johnson not to seek renomination. After the assassination of Robert Kennedy in June of 1968, George McGovern entered the race as a stand-in for his slain friend. Meanwhile, Vice-President Hubert Humphrey picked up the Johnson mantle at the Democratic National Convention in Chicago. Although Humphrey had not run in a single primary, influential state-party leaders supported him and used traditional, but nondemocratic, procedures to wield a disproportionate influence on the convention floor. Through a maneuver called the "unit rule," which bound individual delegates to vote with the preferences of the majority of the state delegation, state-party bosses managed both to give Humphrey the nomination and to defeat an amendment to end the war in Vietnam.

Distraught at what they considered a coup by forces entrenched within the Democratic party, supporters of McCarthy, Kennedy,

At the 1968 Democratic National Convention in Chicago, Senator McGovern addressed the Vietnam forum of war protesters, whose concerns were not heeded by traditional party leaders. Photograph by Dennis Warren

and McGovern worked to remove boss control from future national conventions. Although the insurgents failed to nominate their candidate or pass an amendment to end the war, Chicago did serve as the birthplace of a radical reformation, the effects of which would continue long after the more sensational events in the city's streets had faded. To heal the wounds of the tortuous convention, Humphrey allowed the delegates to vote on the resolution that created the Commission on Party Structure and Delegate Selection. The commission was to study state-party practices to "assure itself that the make-up of [the] party . . . is representative of rank-and-file Democrats" and determine whether "adequate opportunity for grass-roots participation" existed. Because many state-party leaders had chosen their delegations to the 1968 convention more than a year before the primary season, the resolution also urged more timely selection of delegates.[9]

Throughout the presidential campaign of 1968, the party remained divided. While regular Democratic supporters such as organized labor and civil-rights groups worked strenuously for Humphrey's election, insurgent Democrats struggled over whether or not to support the candidate. Backers of Eugene McCarthy indicated that they would not settle for a few lines of reform language in the party bylaws; Humphrey would have to earn their votes. In October, a group of mostly McCarthy supporters created the New Democratic Coalition (NDC). According to the *New York Times*, the goal of the group was to "gain control of the party structure in each state" in addition to pushing for an end to the war in Vietnam.[10] The creation of the NDC illustrated the vital link between party reform and electoral loyalty in the minds of insurgent Democrats. Humphrey recognized this link and sought to placate NDC members and other insurgents with assurances that he was "interested in developing recommendations which will maximize democracy in the nomination process."[11] Although the group failed to endorse Humphrey officially, some NDC members told the *New York Times* that they would support Humphrey but would focus on "the election . . . of liberal candidates to Congress and to state and local offices" in 1968.[12]

The results of the presidential election disheartened all Democrats. Nixon defeated Humphrey by a scant margin in the popular vote, but by more than one hundred electoral votes. Significantly, Alabama governor George Wallace ran a strong third-party candidacy under the American Independent party banner and managed to win the electoral votes of five southern states. Political observers rushed to analyze the election outcome, offering essentially three appraisals. The first, popularized by Kevin Phillips in *The Emerging Republican Majority*, viewed the election as the first among a new Republican alignment that would continue to dominate American politics for the near future. Phillips assumed that Wallace's success represented a rejection of Democratic party, as opposed to establishment, politics. He also argued that Nixon's victory reflected steady Republican gains in the South, leaving the Democrats with reliable voting blocs only in the Northeast. This emerging Republican majority, the author continued, derived essentially from ethnocultural conflicts between blacks and whites, as well as between Catholics and Protestants. Nixon's campaign capitalized on these conflicts, and his victory established a new coalition of Republican blue-collar, white voters that had traditionally made up the Democratic base since the New Deal.[13]

The second appraisal concentrated on the division within the Democratic party brought on by the insurgent opposition to the Vietnam War. Democrats who had consistently supported Lyndon Johnson, and later Hubert Humphrey, blamed the antiwar forces of McCarthy and Kennedy for dividing the party. Leon Keyserling, an ADA executive committee member who had disapproved of the group's endorsement of McCarthy, expressed the exasperation many liberals felt after the election. "Had [Humphrey] staked out new and bold programs," Keyserling believed, he would have received more support from the "dissident" Democrats. By the same token, Keyserling recognized that popular support for social programs had waned. He blamed the decline in popular liberalism on those who had concentrated on ending the war, further dividing the Democratic party. "Liberal organizations," he argued, ". . . had not made the sustained effort necessary to make such programs part and parcel of liberal thinking of the country."[14] In a more blunt appraisal, Richard Daley, mayor of Chicago, blamed the insurgents for the violence perpetrated during the national convention and its negative effect on the voters. "They came [to Chicago] to destroy Johnson," Daley accused, "and in doing that they didn't care whether they destroyed the Democratic Party—and this is what happened."[15]

The insurgent Democrats themselves offered the third analysis of the election, one that would win over a majority of the party by the end of 1970. Speaking for the insurgents, George McGovern explained in an article for *Harper's Magazine* how the party had lost its credibility with the American electorate at Chicago. The rancor over the Vietnam War, he argued, "showed that institutions which work satisfactorily in times considered normal may be unequal to periods of stress." McGovern articulated his belief that the party division was not simply a policy squabble but, rather, the result of the actions of a few party leaders. Beholden to Johnson and Humphrey politically, they had controlled the convention delegates, stifling a majority that wanted to end the war. "Feelings about the war ran so deep," McGovern concluded about the politics of 1968, "that it became impossible to hide the presence of a fundamental defect within the structure of the convention system itself. The defect was a failure of democracy and went to the heart of the American political system."[16]

The varied contemporary analyses of the election of 1968 remain relatively unchanged today. In *Divided They Fell*, for instance, Ronald Radosh elaborates on the arguments of both Kevin Phillips and Richard Daley. He chides the Democrats for not reacting first to the apparent conservative shift among "traditional Democratic blue-collar voters . . . toward the Republican slot." Furthermore, Radosh contends, Democrats failed to "look at the meaning of the results" of the election and caved in to "pressure . . . to push even farther to the political Left."[17] As will become evident, however, the Democratic party not only focused on the significance of the Nixon/Wallace vote but also supported the reform effort (and its ideological consequences) in a conscious effort to improve the party's electoral prospects.

The McGovern Commission

Spurred on by the New Democratic Coalition, both the new Democratic national party chairman, Fred Harris, and the party's titular head, Hubert Humphrey, proceeded with the formation of the twenty-eight-member Commission on Party Structure and Delegate Selection in early 1969. Harris, although a Humphrey supporter in Chicago, was a committed reformer. Nonetheless, his ties to Humphrey convinced the insurgent-led NDC to pressure Harris into naming members who were "committed to party reform and not people who have vested interest in the status quo." The enthusiasm of the NDC for reform was not entirely altruistic, either. The coalition's executive director, Earl Craig, counted on the still-unborn commission to keep its cause alive. "We have to provide a vehicle to express the interests and frustrations of all the people who challenged the party leadership in 1968," he explained. Without that vehicle, Craig worried, "interest will die."[18]

Humphrey and Harris concentrated first on naming a commission chairman. Although Harris would make the official announcement, Humphrey, for all intents and purposes, made the selection. Senator Harold Hughes of Iowa had long championed party reform and publicly offered his services as chairman. Humphrey, however, considered McGovern, not Hughes, to be the best candidate because, according to McGovern, the former vice-president "wanted somebody who had credibility with the reform elements, but also had enough loyalty to the Democratic Party to endorse and campaign" for him. Hughes had not immediately endorsed the Humphrey campaign in 1968, and McGovern recalled that Humphrey considered Hughes "disloyal" and believed the Iowan "hadn't really campaigned for him."[19]

While Humphrey wooed McGovern, the South Dakotan remained cautious about accepting the chairmanship. McGovern had supported the reform resolution at the national convention but maintained that he perceived little political advantage in leading the reform effort. He wanted to run for president in 1972 and knew that the commission would be controversial.[20] Ultimately, however, with the advice of future commission consultant Richard C. Wade, a professor of history at the University of Chicago, McGovern concluded that the position could have political benefits, as well. In Wade's view, the reform issue, if melded with the antiwar issue, could lure back the insurgent forces that had abandoned the party in 1968.[21]

With a chair in place, Fred Harris proceeded to appoint commission members, selecting those with diverse geographic and political interests. But, as political scientist Byron Shafer noted, "the first and most fundamental" criteria for the composition of the commission rested on selecting a majority of members who favored reform.[22] To achieve some balance, Harris also appointed members who had supported the nomination of Humphrey in 1968. For instance, Will Davis, chair of the State Democratic Executive Committee of Texas, and George Mitchell, a national committee member, represented the traditional party structure on the commission. In addition, Harris appointed I. W. Abel, president of the United Steelworkers of America, as one of two labor representatives. AFL-CIO president George Meany, however, persuaded Abel that the commission would prove meaningless, and Abel never attended a meeting. Meany's reaction can be explained on two levels. First, Harris had offended the AFL-CIO in his pursuit of reform. Although labor had worked hard for the Democrats in 1968, the party had placed its future with the insurgents rather than the traditional element. Second, time was on labor's side. Meany and the rest of organized labor had always had de facto veto power in the party. Even if the reforms threatened to undermine their role in local Democratic politics, Meany believed he could exert his considerable influence on the majority of old-line members of the national committee to thwart the reform effort.[23]

As commission chair, McGovern appointed insurgent Democrats to the important staff positions and structured the group so that the reform-minded elements would control the guideline process from the beginning. He created an executive committee, made up of a super majority of pro-reform members, that served as an early sounding board for staff proposals and full commission business. Among others, the executive committee included Harold Hughes; Fred Dutton, a former aide to Robert Kennedy; David Mixner, the youngest and most radical commission member; and Donald Fraser, who would later serve as commission chairman.[24] Even though McGovern organized the commission in the same manner as a congressional committee, which allows subcommittee chairs to control the specifics of legislation, all decisions were forwarded to the executive committee and commission staff for review. In a memo, staff director Robert Nelson suggested to McGovern that the senator needed to make it "clear that final policy considerations are specifically reserved for the full commission."[25] This procedure insured that far-reaching reforms would not be killed in committee.

McGovern convened the first meeting of the Commission on Party Structure and Delegate Selection on 1 March 1969. At that meeting, he and others asserted that comprehensive reforms were the best hope for the Democratic party to regain its electoral majority. The senator reminded commission members that the party had been losing both voters and offices, citing the decline of Democratic governorships from thirty-seven in 1962 to only eighteen by 1969.[26] In particular, he noted, the party was "losing some of its traditional constituency without clear prospects of a new and larger constituency. Our Commission has been told . . . to make recommendations for the cure."[27] Senator Birch Bayh of Indiana agreed and suggested that the real work of the commission lay less in delegate selection than in party structure. "One step that must be considered," Bayh asserted, "is how to get people involved in the actual election process, in addition to the nominating process."[28]

The following month, the commission embarked on an ambitious schedule of hearings in seventeen cities across the country to gather information for its recommendations to the Democratic party. Had Ronald Radosh explored the hearing process in his study, he would have found a logical basis for the commission's ultimate decision to end the traditional influence of bosses and open the party to liberal activists. Certain characteristics marked each hearing and determined the outcome of the commission's final report. First, everyone who testified began his or her statement with an endorsement of reform. Second, the make-up of the witness pool was skewed overwhelmingly toward insurgent Democrats. The absence of regular national party members and labor representatives meant that the insurgents overwhelmed proponents of moderate reform. Finally, most witnesses called for an increased participation of youth in party affairs, testifying overwhelmingly that the party had to reform itself and recruit new, young members in order to elect Democrats to office.[29]

The commission convened the first hearing in Washington, D.C., in late April 1969. Unlike the hearings that followed, national politicians dominated this event and, after expressing their support for the commission's work, defended the regular wing of the party. Hubert Humphrey, who did not attend, endorsed reform but reminded insurgent Democrats that "to be 'regular' is not necessarily to be wrong." Humphrey's running mate in the 1968 election, Edmund Muskie of Maine, conveyed a similar message. "It is not enough," he commented, "to suggest that our problems can be solved by changing the guard from one 'establishment' to another."[30] Neither titular leader, however, suggested any particular course of action to heal the party's wounds.

The commission's work received similarly lukewarm responses from other traditional Democrats, who appeared in smaller numbers at later hearings. In fact, most critics of the reform effort, like the AFL-CIO, did not participate. Discussing this problem during a meeting in May, the executive committee concluded that the "regulars do not feel the necessity, obligation, or even justification to testify."[31] Like most Democratic party regulars, Humphrey believed the party already offered sufficient opportunity for insurgents to participate. In his written testimony at the commission hearing in Washington, he unconvincingly suggested that the first duty of a "regular party stalwart" was "to keep the door open" for anyone who wanted to participate in the system.[32] Humphrey's complacency typified that of many regular Democrats. To them the 1968 election was an aberration, not a harbinger of future Democratic defeats. The party simply had to refine its message, not reform its traditions, to appeal to those who had elected Richard Nixon or voted for George Wallace.

In the view of McGovern and other reformers, however, the party had lost not simply because Democrats were voting for Republicans, but because past and future Democrats were opting out of the party altogether. Insurgent Democrats and New Left college students did not constitute the entirety of this group, either. George Wallace's showing in 1968, for instance, indicated that his support could not be defined as exclusively conservative. At least one member of the McGovern Commission staff recognized this dynamic in 1969. In response to an article contending that the commission was "perfectly content to wash off the rolls the millions of conservative Democrats who voted for George Wallace last

November," an unidentified staff member lamented the author's "failure to understand why lots of people voted for Wallace—i.e. profound alienation and conservative."[33]

To address the discontent that had surfaced in 1968, the Mc-Govern Commission sought to appeal to young voters, who represented not only the most alienated and disillusioned segment of the electorate, but also the most promising and tangible target for the Democratic party. Shortly after his tenure with the commission, Fred Dutton published a book that detailed many of the assumptions that lay behind the commission's focus on youth. In *Changing Sources of Power: American Politics in the 1970s,* Dutton held that a new generation of affluent, well-educated, active elites would, if properly nurtured by the Democratic party, usher in a revolution in politics comparable to the New Deal revolution of the 1930s. Like the immigrants who came of age during the early decades of the century, the baby-boom generation appeared to be a rich source of electoral energy. "Franklin Roosevelt brought into the electorate of the 1930s a large number of older urban poor," Dutton argued. "The political involvement of the young will similarly be sharply raised during the years ahead."[34] Though he did not explicitly call for reform of institutions like the Democratic party, Dutton explained, "The real revolt is against government, mass politics . . . and long-prevailing liberal methods. That is why . . . much of [this generation] has fastened onto the concept of 'participatory democracy.'"[35] The McGovern Commission, then, sought to gain what support it could muster from this group by opening up the party at the state and local level and taking power away from party bosses.

Many who testified at the regional hearings of the commission in 1969 viewed youth as the foundation for revitalizing the Democratic party. "Without significant reform," warned James Loeb, an executive-committee member of the Americans for Democratic Action, "the Party may not gain the loyalties of the millions of young new voters and the additional millions of older voters in ghettos, barrios, suburbs, and universities whose participation in 1968 made history."[36] Percy Sutton, president of the Manhattan Borough of the Democratic party, argued for a "new coalition of the poor, the oppressed minority groups, the young, the liberals, the new day-type labor unions." This coalition "must be embraced," he implored, "within a new form of Democratic Party structure, one which will supplant the present political club structure."[37]

On 19 and 20 November 1969, McGovern reconvened the entire commission to decide on final guidelines. The sessions focused on the minutiae of both delegate selection and party structure. McGovern started the 19 November session with a flourish, introducing the most controversial guidelines first. The initial two contained language that supported a balanced representation of blacks, women, and youth in every convention delegation. To strengthen the measures, Fred Dutton proposed that each state delegation be required to have a representation of the three groups that was proportional to their numbers in the state's population. By mandating that the make-up of each delegation reflect the state's inhabitants at large, Dutton hoped to ensure their participation both at the convention and in daily party business. Opposition flared immediately. Will Davis of Texas, for instance, called the Dutton proposal "absurd" for allowing the national party to dictate the composition of each state's convention delegation.[38] For his part, McGovern tried to ease the disagreement by proposing that the commission merely urge, rather than require, the state committees to adopt proportional representation.[39]

Upon McGovern's suggestion, Katherine Peden, who had run unsuccessfully for the United States Senate from Kentucky, quickly raised her concerns. "I think for us to back down . . . on the position of women [and youth]," she explained, "would be just as substantial a mistake as . . . if we had backed down on race." McGovern offered that he had "no problem voting for the strongest possible language" and proceeded to call the question on Dutton's language requiring the compliance of the state parties.[40] The commission adopted Dutton's proposal by a vote of thirteen to seven. In general, the members who favored the idea reasoned that state parties had to be forced into diversifying by some means and that proportional representation was the best method available. The de facto quota language sparked criticism immediately within the commission and later among neoconservatives. Norman Podhoretz, for example, assailed the doctrine that lay behind the decision as the "New Politics ideal of a society based on equality of condition [as opposed to one] based on equality of opportunity."[41]

By 20 November, the commission had decided on all its guidelines for integrating a broader sampling of the electorate into party affairs. The bulk of the recommendations were less controversial and included requiring adequate public notice of party meetings and prohibiting discriminatory voter registration, unreasonable costs and fees, and premature delegate selection. The commission also banned rules and practices that permitted undue influence on delegates, such as proxy voting, the unit rule, and winner-take-all primaries. The lone exception to the winner-take-all prohibition was California, whose state party had supported McGovern's brief run for the presidential nomination in 1968. Fred Dutton, a native Californian, "privately . . . reminded party liberals and antiwar leaders," McGovern confessed, "that in 1972 California would probably support a presidential contender representing their strongest concerns."[42] In other words, Dutton convinced McGovern that the insurgent element in his state could deliver California's 271 delegates to its favorite. The potential prize proved too tempting to the aspiring presidential candidate, and in the end, commission members allowed the California exception until the 1976 convention. The McGovern Commission announced its final guidelines in a report entitled *Mandate for Reform* in the spring of 1970.

Echoing the comments of Norman Podhoretz, historian Ronald Radosh calls the reforms a "radical reinterpretation of the traditional view that supported equality of opportunity for all Americans, once the mainstay of the Democrats' approach toward politics."[43] Clearly, the practical effect of the reforms would be less dubious. The changes in party structure and the subsequent dispersal of local- and state-party influence produced two distinct results, both beneficial to the Democratic party. First, the commission's work co-opted the concerns of insurgent groups that had not supported Hubert Humphrey's candidacy in 1968, thus rendering their opposition mute in future elections. Second, the reforms encouraged the participation of young Democrats, who worked diligently for the party in the midterm election of 1970.

Their efforts helped elect an unexpectedly large number of Democrats to state and national offices.

Before the fall elections, however, the need to bring young people into the party, which had been voiced repeatedly throughout the 1969 hearings, drove McGovern to convene a special Youth Participation Subcommittee of the Commission on Party Structure and Delegate Selection in July 1970. McGovern's prefatory remarks reflected both the reliance he had placed on the energy of young voters and the need for the Democrats to rejuvenate the disillusioned. "However open the process," he declared, "if the product does not provide progressive answers to the problems that concern young people, our Party—and any other party—starts to be rejected."[44] Fearing McGovern's words to be true, Larry O'Brien, who replaced Fred Harris as chairman of the Democratic National Committee in February 1970, offered a reformed Democratic party as the best option to young voters. Calling the commission reforms "the most drastic ever to sweep a political party in this country," O'Brien implored, "*this* is what we have to offer the young people seeking a place in the political process."[45]

Significantly, the subcommittee concentrated on more than participation. The potential political power of new voters shared, if not stole, the spotlight during the proceedings, as attention continually returned to the role the rising generation of voters would play in gaining Democratic victory in future elections. In preparing for earlier hearings, McGovern had requested statistics on recently enfranchised young voters in England. The results confirmed the wisdom of the reform path. Among the findings, the Opinion Research Centre of London reported that 70 percent of English youth had registered to vote and that young people were more likely to vote for political fringe candidates and to choose the Labour party over the Conservative party.[46] The English experience, in other words, boded well for a Democratic party that encouraged broad political participation and simultaneously moved left of center. Edward Schneider, founder of the Movement for a New Congress, cited the results of recent special elections in the United States to affirm that the electoral energy of young people could make the difference in close elections if the Democratic candidate was sufficiently progressive. While noting that students "are turning away from the old politics, a break with the system they have grown to suspect," he testified that the work of young Democratic activists "can produce a 2–6% point gain for the candidates they support."[47]

However, before the participation of young voters and the other changes called for in the commission's *Mandate for Reform* could affect national politics on the scale that McGovern and other like-minded Democrats anticipated, the Democratic National Committee had to approve it and agree to make the guidelines party law in each of the states. When O'Brien became national committee chair, some insurgents had expressed concern that his "old politics" pedigree might incline him against the reform guidelines, but O'Brien had dispelled that fear quickly. "We cannot achieve victory in the future," he commented in July, "while torn by the divisions of the past. To win, we simply *must change*."[48] With O'Brien's acquiescence, Byron Shafer contended, "the alternative Democratic coalition had been given new, major, and unexpected assets" within the party.[49] Early in 1971, the Democratic National Committee incorporated the McGovern Commission's guidelines into its Call to the 1972 convention, thus setting the convention rules.[50]

Consequences

Because many insurgent Democrats distrusted O'Brien and his ties to traditional party elements, extra-party groups had worked alongside the commission to push for party reform. The New Democratic Coalition, founded on the heels of the disastrous 1968 convention, played the largest role in such ventures. It had pressured Fred Harris to name the McGovern Commission shortly after the election of 1968, and it acted as the commission's grass-roots arm during the early months of the commission's existence. The organization not only participated enthusiastically in the commission's hearing process but also helped to elect a number of Democrats to state and national office. In fourteen states, local NDC chapters had directly aided the Democratic party in campaigns. Even so, by early 1970, the NDC was in disarray, lacking both a leader and an overriding issue on which to concentrate.

In the end, the success of the reform process—not ideological extremism, as Ronald Radosh argues—killed the NDC.[51] Harold Hughes suggested as much when he addressed the group in Chicago early in 1970 and argued that "the Democratic Party's efforts to reform itself offered hope for the future." Coalition founder Eugene McCarthy, who had left the organization, agreed that the national party's progress on reform had usurped the NDC mission and commented that the party was "beginning to look like the party that I was describing back in 1968."[52]

Indicating that others still saw party reform as an ongoing process, Stephen Schlesinger started publishing the *New Democrat*, a "political journal for progressive ideas within the [Democratic] Party," in 1970.[53] The implementation of the McGovern Commission reforms was the focal point of the magazine, which suspended publication upon McGovern's nomination as the Democratic presidential candidate in July 1972. The October 1970 issue of the *New Democrat* presented comments on reform and the future of the party from eighteen young activist Democrats, including Schlesinger himself, who feared that a faction of the insurgents of 1968 would form a fourth party by 1972. "To co-opt that movement," he argued, "the Democratic leadership must implement a thorough reform program." Curtis Gans, a McCarthy aide, commented that the Democratic party needed to "complete the task of reforming itself . . . and emerge in 1972 with a leader." Others, such as McGovern Commission consultant Richard Wade, argued directly for George McGovern's ascension to that role. "If there is not change in the party," Wade maintained, "the result would be an easy Nixon-Agnew victory. The best guarantee against this is a reformed Democratic Party." He went on to compliment former Kennedy and McCarthy activists who had worked hard in the reform effort and urged them to continue. "Then, perhaps," he suggested, "[they might] nominate the man who now best embodies that effort, the Senator from South Dakota."[54]

As the midterm elections of 1970 approached, politicians and political pundits renewed their interest in the American electorate. Early in the year, Richard Scammon and Ben Wattenberg published *The Real Majority*, a new study on American politics, which found that conservative social issues, such as law and order, had engulfed the political landscape and that a renewed liberalism was not what the public craved.[55] In tandem with the Scammon/ Wattenberg findings, voter apathy and a general dissatisfaction with politics offered the Republican party a unique opportunity to consolidate the gains of 1968 in the congressional elections of 1970. No party of the incumbent president had gained seats in both the House and Senate in a midterm election since 1934. As the possibility of such a pivotal election approached, the progressive-leaning editors of the *New York Times* warned in October 1970 against "the tragic aspect of such an outcome." While stating that "there is no way of telling whether 1970 will be a year of political upheaval," the editors conceded, "preliminary evidence about the election must be encouraging to President Nixon."[56] The Republicans, acting on this evidence as well, targeted members with liberal or reformist voting records during the campaign season. At a rally in Arkansas in early October, Vice-President Spiro Agnew attacked McGovern, among others, and the attempts to reform the Democratic party. "Men like Kennedy, McGovern, [Fred] Harris, and Birch Bayh, who have sought to give respectability to radical liberalism," Agnew intoned, "shall answer to history for what they have done to the Democratic party."[57]

The combination of Republican acrimony and the findings in *The Real Majority* concerned many liberals. After a particularly critical radio editorial aired in his home state of Indiana, Senator Vance Hartke wrote to Joseph Rauh, worried that his endorsement from the liberal Americans for Democratic Action would cost him his seat in 1970.[58] In response to such concerns, the ADA issued its members a call to action early in the year. Warning that liberal politicians may "bend before the conservative wind," the memo suggested that "effective, progressive forces" composed of "new young political activists" willing to rally behind issues such as "peace, environment, . . . hunger and poverty and [reformed] participation within the political system" needed to come to the rescue by supplementing grassroots networks and helping local Democrats.[59]

The congressional and gubernatorial elections of 1970 provided evidence that the conservative wind had not filled the Republican sails. Moreover, the results indicated that grassroots efforts of the kind the ADA had relied upon, and the McGovern Commission reforms had intended, had achieved substantial, though not overwhelming, success at the ballot box. While the Democrats lost four seats in the Senate, Vance Hartke retained his Senate seat in Indiana. In addition, Democrats picked up ten governorships across the country and twelve seats in the House of Representatives, resulting in a freshman class of thirty-two Democrats.[60] The results of the midterm elections caused those who had relied on the "real majority" to win elections to take pause. Referring to Kevin Phillips's 1969 book *The Emerging Republican Majority*, R. W. Apple, Jr., of the *New York Times* mockingly called 1970 "the year of the non-emerging Republican majority," noting that the harsh assaults on liberalism had backfired on many Republicans. "For the Democrats," Apple wrote, "life suddenly looks a good deal more pleasant."[61] Indeed it did. According to *Congressional Quarterly,* much of the Democratic success could be pinned on student campaign workers. Citing the Movement for a New Congress, which had appeared in the wake of the Kent State shootings, the journal found an unusual number of motivated young people "determined to elect peace-oriented candidates to Congress."[62]

The gubernatorial results proved most encouraging to the insurgent wing of the party. All ten Democratic candidates who replaced incumbent Republican governors had acted in sympathy with the national party reforms. As Byron Shafer commented, governors were "likely to desire political understandings with constituents who *were* sympathetic to reform. . . . These [constituents] had representatives in the state legislature; they were often directly relevant to the success or failure of his policy initiatives; they might even have significant representation in the state party itself."[63]

Shafer and other writers were not as quick to find the same results in the congressional elections, however. Even so, McGovern and other reformers could take heart that the class of 1970 represented a growing trend within the party. Thirty-two new Democratic members of Congress entered the House in January of 1971, approximately one-third of whom had won in districts formerly represented by a Republican. More significantly, their voting record during their first session reflected the politics of the insurgent forces of 1968. For example, the membership voted on two rather blatant efforts to stop the war in Vietnam. One sought to remove the military draft power of the president, while the other proposed to cut off funding for military activity in Indochina after 31 December 1971. Both votes, not surprisingly, fell to defeat by a large margin. Of the fifty-two Democratic votes for the amendment to end the draft, however, fourteen came from freshmen. And of the seventy-five votes to end funding for the war by the end of the year, sixteen came from the new class, or half of the freshmen, all of whom voted. Although these results do not point to a definitive ideology among the new members, the freshmen supported both measures at a greater rate than did their more experienced brethren.[64]

A resolution to reduce taxes also revealed a break between the new class and the older members. Normally, any measure to reduce taxes, especially one contained within a resolution rather than a bill, receives overwhelming support from legislators. While this resolution passed easily, sixty-six Democrats voted against it. Among these members, fourteen—or almost half of the twenty-nine freshmen who voted on the measure—voted with the minority.[65] Whether they voted against the measure because it was worded improperly or because it interfered with their hopes of renewed governmental programs is not clear. Unquestionably, however, the new Democratic members voted in a more liberal manner relative to their party peers and, to that extent, suggested the future of the Democratic party politics.

Freshened by their success in the midterm election, Democrats looked optimistically toward the next presidential campaign. In July 1970, McGovern had called a meeting of his close advisors at his farmhouse in Cedar Point, Maryland, to plan a strategy to win the party's nomination. Among the conferees were his eventual campaign director Gary Hart, reform commission staffer Richard Stearns, and commission consultant Richard Wade. While conceding that he might be the most "left-leaning candidate," McGovern believed himself to be the "most reconciling candidate," as well.[66] McGovern recognized that the reform movement had not completely healed the wounds of 1968, but he still considered it possible that he might unify the party behind its tenets, and he stunned his Democratic opponents during the primary campaign in 1972. However, the division within the party, coupled with the astute maneuverings of the Nixon Administration, ultimately prevented McGovern from winning in November.

Historian Ronald Radosh correctly indicates that the McGovern Commission and its impact on party politics stemmed directly from the schism within the Democratic party. However, Radosh holds the insurgent Democrats' reform effort responsible for the party's failure to win the presidency in 1972 and beyond. The reforms, he concludes, "diminished [the Democratic party's] breadth and gave more power to extremely liberal activists who were unrepresentative of the party's membership at large."[67] It is difficult to argue against such an assertion made with the benefit of hindsight. After all, the Republicans dominated presidential politics from 1968 until 1992. On the other hand, as political historian Allan Lichtman has asserted in his work examining the historical patterns of presidential elections since the 1850s, no Democratic presidential contender was likely to have emerged victorious in 1972, 1980, 1984, or 1988 given the course of events leading up to the elections. In the specific case of 1972, when Republicans failed to gain control of either house of Congress, the "anticipated realignment of the American electorate" toward conservatism failed to materialize. In fact, Lichtman argues, "Nixon managed to preserve his own incumbency only by adroit maneuvering in economic and foreign policy late in the term."[68]

Whatever the relationship between the Democrats' reform efforts and their subsequent election disappointments, the real question is whether they pursued the most logical course of action available to them at the time. After the election of 1968, the party had a choice: it could reform in an effort to unify, or it could do nothing and risk further splintering. The consequences of having done nothing prior to 1968 were a raucous national convention, deep party divisions, and a Nixon victory. The consequences of reform were unknown in January of 1969. In the months that followed, the party formulated and acted on a plan to attract the growing number of alienated voters and disenfranchised youth. Essentially, the reform guidelines accomplished the goal they had set out to achieve. First, they allowed for more primaries to be held so that rank-and-file Democrats could vote for their presidential preference instead of having it dictated to them by party officials. Second, they allowed new opinions that had been muffled in 1968 to enter into the national political debate. As of November 1970, the Democratic party managed to attract active, young voters, succeeded in quelling insurgent opposition, and elected significant numbers of new Democratic officeholders. Indeed, in the results of the midterm election of 1970 and as the next presidential election approached, the decision to reform the party appeared, if not a political masterstroke, an effective and intelligent response to the chaos that had afflicted the party not two years earlier.

NOTES

The author presented a summary of this essay at the Symposium for George McGovern, sponsored by the Eisenhower Center, University of New Orleans, on 8 April 1997, at the National Archives Building in Washington, D.C.

1. Byron E. Shafer, *Quiet Revolution: The Struggle for the Democratic Party and the Shaping of Post-Reform Politics* (New York: Russell Sage Foundation, 1983), pp. 541–45; Jeane Kirkpatrick, *The New Presidential Elite: Men and Women in American Politics* (New York: Russell Sage Foundation and The Twentieth Century Fund, 1976), pp. 42–43; Norman Podhoretz, *Breaking Ranks: A Political Memoir* (New York: Harper & Row, 1979), pp. 339–40; Thomas Byrne Edsall, *The New Politics of Inequality* (New York: W. W. Norton & Co., 1984), pp. 49–53.

2. ". . . the Defeat . . .," *New York Times*, 9 Nov. 1972, p. 46.

3. Theodore H. White, *The Making of the President, 1972* (New York: Atheneum Publishers, 1973), p. 341.

4. Kirkpatrick, *New Presidential Elite*, pp. 41, 328; Podhoretz, *Breaking Ranks*, pp. 339–44; Edsall, *New Politics*, pp. 63, 66.

5. Ronald Radosh, *Divided They Fell: The Demise of the Democratic Party, 1964–1996* (New York: Free Press, 1996), p. 138.

6. *See* William Cavala and Austin Ranney, "Changing the Rules Changes the Game," *American Political Science Review* 68 (Mar. 1974): 42; James I. Lengle and Byron Shafer, "Primary Rules, Political Power, and Social Change," *American Political Science Review* 70 (Mar. 1976): 25–26; Nelson W. Polsby, *Consequences of Party Reform* (New York: Oxford University Press, 1983), pp. 160–66.

7. Resolution, Americans for Democratic Action, National Board

Meeting, 10 Feb. 1968, Americans for Democratic Action File, 1968–1969, Papers of Joseph Rauh, Library of Congress, Washington, D.C.

8. Keynote speech, Don Edwards to Conference of Concerned Democrats, 2 Dec. 1967, Democratic Party Democratic Peace Caucus File, September-December 1967, ibid.

9. Joseph Foote, ed., *The Presidential Nominating Conventions, 1968* (Washington, D.C.: Congressional Quarterly Service, 1968), p. 200.

10. Donald Janson, "Rebellious Democrats Establish Coalition to Seek Party Reform," *New York Times*, 7 Oct. 1968, p. 40.

11. Quoted in Shafer, *Quiet Revolution*, p. 45.

12. Janson, "Rebellious Democrats," p. 40.

13. *See* Kevin P. Phillips, *The Emerging Republican Majority* (New Rochelle, N.Y.: Arlington House, 1969).

14. Memorandum, Keyserling to Marvin Rosenberg, 10 Nov. 1968, Americans for Democratic Action File, 1968–1970, Rauh Papers.

15. Hearing, Chicago, 7 June 1969, Hearings: Special Testimony File, Democratic National Committee (DNC) Papers, Presidential Libraries, National Archives, Washington, D.C.

16. George McGovern, "The Lessons of 1968," *Harper's Magazine* 240 (Jan. 1970): 43–47.

17. Radosh, *Divided They Fell*, p. 134.

18. Quoted in Steven V. Roberts, "Democratic Group Battling to Keep Alive 'New Politics' of '68," *New York Times*, 28 Dec. 1968, p. 17.

19. Interview with George McGovern, 23 Jan. 1993, Washington, D.C.

20. Ibid.

21. Shafer, *Quiet Revolution*, p. 62.

22. Ibid., p. 57.

23. Ibid., pp. 92–94.

24. McGovern named Robert Nelson, former aide to Harold Hughes, staff director; Eli Segal, a former McCarthy aide, chief counsel; and Ken Bode, who had served as McGovern's floor manager at the 1968 Democratic convention, director of research. In addition, he appointed Richard Wade, who had convinced McGovern of the political potential of the commission, to a consultant's position. George S. McGovern, *Grassroots: The Autobiography of George McGovern* (New York: Random House, 1977), pp. 136–38.

25. Confidential memorandum, Nelson to McGovern, 5 Mar. 1969, Inter-staff Memos File—Real, DNC Papers.

26. Minutes, McGovern-Fraser Commission, 1 Mar. 1969, Recommendations: Rank-and-File File, ibid.

27. Opening statement, McGovern to McGovern-Fraser Commission, 1 Mar. 1969, McGovern Speeches File, ibid.

28. Minutes, McGovern-Fraser Commission, 1 Mar. 1969.

29. For witnesses and testimony offered at various locations, *see* Hearings: Special Testimony File, DNC Papers.

30. Hearing, Washington, D.C., 25 Apr. 1969, ibid.

31. Minutes, Executive Committee meeting, 26 May 1969, Recommendations: Rank-and-File File, ibid.

32. Hearing, Washington, D.C., 25 Apr. 1969.

33. Note written on Jerry Green, editorial, *New York Daily News*, 27 Apr. 1969, Hearings: Special Testimony, Clippings File, DNC Papers.

34. Frederick G. Dutton, *Changing Sources of Power: American Politics in the 1970s* (New York: McGraw-Hill Book Co., 1971), p. 20.

35. Ibid., p. 49.

36. Commission hearing testimony, Washington, D.C., 25 Apr. 1969, Washington Hearing File, DNC Papers.

37. Commission hearing, New York City, 3 May 1969, New York Hearing File, ibid.

38. Transcript, McGovern Commission meeting, 19 Nov. 1969, Recommendations: Rank-and-File File, ibid.

39. Shafer, *Quiet Revolution*, pp. 170–71.

40. Tape transcript, quoted ibid., p. 171.

41. Podhoretz, *Breaking Ranks*, p. 344.

42. McGovern, *Grassroots*, p. 150.

43. Radosh, *Divided They Fell*, p. 144.

44. Testimony, Subcommittee on Youth Participation, 29 July 1970, Youth Hearing Testimony File, DNC Papers.

45. Ibid.

46. Humphrey Taylor to McGovern, 20 July 1969, Youth Hearing Correspondence File, DNC Papers.

47. Hearing, Youth Participation Subcommittee, 29 July 1970, Youth Hearing Testimony File, ibid.

48. Ibid.

49. Shafer, *Quiet Revolution*, p. 243.

50. McGovern, *Grassroots*, p. 151.

51. Minutes, Executive Committee, 19 Mar. 1969, Recommendations: Rank-and-File File, DNC Papers; Steven V. Roberts, "For Former Supporters of McCarthy and Kennedy, New Politics Is a Many-Splintered Thing," *New York Times*, 5 Oct. 1969, p. 68; R. W. Apple, Jr., "Coalition of 1968 Ponders Its Role," *New York Times*, 15 Feb. 1970, p. 26; Radosh, *Divided They Fell*, p. 136.

52. Quoted in R. W. Apple, Jr., "Coalition of 1968 Ponders Its Role,"
p. 26.

53. Stephen C. Schlesinger, *The New Reformers: Forces for Change in American Politics* (Boston: Houghton Mifflin Co., 1975), p. 4.

54. "Thoughts on a Fourth Party," *New Democrat* (Oct. 1970): 1–7, Presidential Campaign File, 1972, Rauh Papers.

55. *See* Richard M. Scammon and Ben J. Wattenberg, *The Real Majority* (New York: Coward-McCann, 1970). The book also served the purposes of later neoconservative pundits, such as Radosh, who argued that the Democrats should have solicited the support of social conservatives instead of adherents of the New Left.

56. "A Pivotal Election," *New York Times*, 4 Oct. 1970, sec. 4, p. 16.

57. James T. Naughton, "7 Democrats Get Agnew Challenge," *New York Times*, 9 Oct. 1970, p. 49.

58. Hartke to Rauh, 14 Apr. 1970, Americans for Democratic Action File, 1968–1970, Rauh Papers.

59. "A Proposal for 1970, Congressional Action Now," ibid.

60. John L. Moore, ed., *Congressional Quarterly's Guide to U.S. Elections*, 2d ed. (Washington, D.C.: Congressional Quarterly, 1985), pp. 456, 1124; Norman J. Ornstein, Thomas E. Mann, and Michael J. Malbin, eds., *Vital Statistics on Congress, 1989–1990* (Washington, D.C., Congressional Quarterly, 1990), pp. 54–55.

61. R. W. Apple, Jr., "What Vote Meant—Nixon Must Change to Survive," *New York Times*, 8 Nov. 1970, sec. 4, p. 1.

62. "Youthful Volunteers Aid Dozens of 1970 Campaigns," *Congressional Quarterly* 28 (28 Oct. 1970): 2691.

63. Shafer, *Quiet Revolution*, p. 305.

64. Robert A. Diamond, ed., *Congressional Quarterly Almanac: 92nd congress, 1st Session, 1971* (Washington, D.C.: Congressional Quarterly, 1972), pp. 8-H, 9-H, 32-H, 33-H.

65. Diamond, ed., *Congressional Quarterly Almanac, 1971*, p. 73.

66. Quoted in White, *Making of the President*, p. 43.

67. Radosh, *Divided They Fell*, pp. xii–xiii.

68. Allan J. Lichtman and Ken DeCell, *The Thirteen Keys to the Presidency* (New York: Madison Books, 1990), p. 352.

CHAPTER SEVEN

A CLEAR CHOICE

GEORGE MCGOVERN AND THE

1972 PRESIDENTIAL RACE

JON D. SCHAFF

George McGovern's political life both prepared him for and pointed him towards a run at the presidency. A World War II veteran, he served in the Kennedy Administration and the United States Senate and spearheaded efforts to reform the national Democratic party. An underdog candidate in 1972, Mc-Govern defied the odds by gaining his party's nomination. But what should have been the pinnacle of a great career turned into an overwhelming defeat at the hands of incumbent president Richard M. Nixon. How did such a devastating defeat occur? How did President Nixon, who had barely won in 1968 and certainly was his own worst enemy, win such an easy victory? Why did a sitting senator, who had the credentials for the presidency, find it so difficult to gain the support of the American people against a flawed opponent? Born of great idealism, the McGovern run for the White House in 1972 is a story of the harsh realities of democratic politics. Yet, while McGovern's reach may have exceeded his grasp, the candidacy was not without its fruits.

Grassroots

After his brief attempt to secure the Democratic nomination at the 1968 Democratic National Convention, it did not take George McGovern long to decide that a quest for the presidency in 1972 was in order. As early as 1969, the senator was spending almost half his time on the road, mostly speaking on college campuses about his opposition to the continuing war in Vietnam, the "excessive outlays for military overkill," and "the neglect of our central cities." McGovern stressed, for example, "the need to employ more of our people in such enterprises as the building of a modern rail and mass-transit system."[1] The warm reception from students across the nation only whetted McGovern's appetite for a presidential run. Discussions with friends and advisers convinced him that he had something to add and a chance to win.

As chair of the committee overseeing the rewriting of his party's nomination rules, McGovern knew that the emphasis being put on primaries and a more diverse delegation at the 1972 convention suited someone like himself who was not part of the party establishment. In the 1972 nomination battle, 60 percent of delegates were chosen by primary voters, as opposed to only 18 percent in 1968. While certainly a Democrat in good standing, McGovern was increasingly identifying with the voices of protest in the nation and in his party. In 1968, it had been the entrenched power in the Democratic party that had handed the nomination to Hubert Humphrey in Richard Daley's Chicago. In 1972, there was hope that a candidate could appeal directly to the people and gain the nomination with or without the backing of party regulars or important gatekeepers such as the labor unions.[2]

The tragedy of Chappaquiddick undermined Senator Edward Kennedy's candidacy for the 1972 race. With no obvious candidate in sight, McGovern decided to announce early so that he could stand alone as the Democratic candidate attacking President Nixon. McGovern made what at that time was the earliest presidential candidacy announcement in history on 18 January 1971, twenty months before the election. Speaking that day from Sioux Falls, South Dakota, the senator said that his campaign would be based on trust, as "people no longer believe what their leaders tell them." The population could no longer depend, he continued, on "those who seek power by back-room deals, coalitions of self-interest, or a continual effort to adjust their policies and beliefs to every seeming shift in public sentiment."[3]

McGovern, however, was not seen by political wise men as a real contender. When Senator Edmund Muskie of Maine declared his candidacy later in 1971, he quickly became the front runner. Muskie gobbled up endorsements from party leaders and gained an early edge in the battle for finances. McGovern, running a grassroots campaign with a tight budget, decided to concentrate on key early primary races. The South Dakota senator and his team, headed by Gary Hart of Colorado, quickly made up an "A list" and "B list" of states in which they could be competitive. High on the A list were the states of New Hampshire and Wisconsin. Like George W. Bush facing John McCain in the Republican race of 2000, Muskie would learn that endorsements are no substitute for pressing the flesh in small states such as New Hampshire. While Muskie traversed the nation picking up endorsements, McGovern worked the voters of New Hampshire one by one.

As the South Dakotan made quiet headway, the Muskie endorsement campaign was earning the attention of the media. In January 1972, *Time* magazine proclaimed Muskie "Nixon's most likely 1972 opponent," putting him ahead of candidates such as Senator Hubert H. Humphrey of Minnesota, Senator Henry ("Scoop") Jackson of Washington, Representative Shirley Chisholm of New York, Governor George Wallace of Alabama, and Mayor John Lindsay of New York City.[4] A month later, *Time* pronounced Muskie the front runner in five of six regions of the country, with the South being Wallace and Jackson country.[5] McGovern, described "as dry as last year's cornstalk" when on the hustings, was widely viewed as Robert Kennedy or Eugene McCarthy without the charisma. He was not favored to win a single primary.[6]

On 7 March 1972, the voters of New Hampshire went to the polls; when the dust settled, Edmund Muskie had won with 48 percent of the vote, but he lost the great expectations game. Running as a native son from neighboring Maine, Muskie was disappointed to receive less than 50 percent of the vote, and his unspectacular showing looked like a qualified win at best. McGovern told the *New York Times*, "It's not the sort of victory [Muskie] imagined."[7] The South Dakotan, on the other hand, shocked the press and political pundits by capturing 37 percent of the vote. The results in New Hampshire showed that the "George McGovern's a nice guy but he can't win" assumption was false, the candidate claimed.[8] McGovern had simply outworked Muskie, who was also hurt by an overly emotional reaction to a newspaper attack on his wife that made some voters question whether he had the character to be president. More substantively, Muskie had remained vague on the issues, preferring to sit on what he thought was a national lead, while McGovern took bold stances on the war, on aid to the poor, and on the environment. Muskie increasingly looked like an empty suit; McGovern was the man with the bold ideas that electrified and mobilized voters. "Sometimes I see seven sides to a question because there are seven sides," Muskie had said, but it was not the kind of statement that might rally the increasingly radical Democratic base.[9]

McGovern did not do as well in the Florida primary, which Wallace won based on his opposition to busing, but the senator did finish second to Muskie in Illinois. The contest then turned to Wisconsin, a state considered crucial by the McGovern team. Here, the contest pitted the South Dakotan against another near native son, Hubert Humphrey of neighboring Minnesota. Muskie, a man of Polish descent, also had the advantage of appealing to the large Polish population of the Milwaukee area. But once again McGovern's rabid grassroots volunteers, described as a "guerrilla army," paved the way to stunning success.[10] McGovern scored a clear victory with a 30-percent plurality, solidly beating Humphrey and relegating Muskie to a humiliating fourth place behind Wallace. The South Dakotan even beat Muskie in the Polish neighborhoods. With a coalition of voters in Wisconsin that was both deep and wide (about a third of his total came from Republicans), George McGovern had to be taken seriously by the nation.[11]

McGovern continued to pile up delegates in states like Vermont, Massachusetts, and Pennsylvania. Short on delegates and money, Muskie bowed out of the race after the Pennsylvania contest. The race appeared to be between McGovern and Humphrey, with California as the big prize and Wallace in the spoiler's role. Humphrey began to attack McGovern as radical and out of step with "regular" Democrats. In Nebraska, in a primary that McGovern would win, Humphrey operatives accused McGovern of being "pro-marijuana, pro-abortion and pro-amnesty for draft resisters."[12] Wallace was felled by a would-be assassin in late May, leaving Humphrey and McGovern to battle it out in California on the sixth of June. In televised debates, Humphrey continued to assail McGovern as weak on defense and culturally out of step with Democrats. The attacks damaged the senator, perhaps for good in the eyes of many, but they were not enough to stop the McGovern juggernaut. The South Dakotan had 153 local headquarters in California to Humphrey's 39 and outspent the "happy warrior" $2 million to $500,000. McGovern again won a plurality of votes and, in the winner-take-all California primary, he walked away with the entire California delegation and seemingly the Democratic nomination.[13]

The Convention

George McGovern had opposed the California system of allocating all of its delegates to the plurality winner of its primary when the party nomination rules were being rewritten but had agreed to postpone its demise until 1976. Concurrently, Hubert Humphrey had said that anyone who challenged the system after the fact should be labeled a "spoilsport." Now that McGovern was set to win the Democratic nomination, however, Humphrey was willing to play the role of spoilsport.[14] The battle over the California delegation would prove to be one of many problems plaguing the Democratic National Convention held in early July in Miami, where the new delegation rules certainly made an impact. In 1968, 5.5 percent of the delegation had been black, 13 percent female, and only 4 percent had been under the age of thirty. In 1972, when the dust settled, 15 percent of Democratic delegates in Miami were black, 36 percent were female, and 22 percent were under thirty. At the same time, union representation was down from the four years previous.[15] It was not a clean and easy process, however.

The new Democratic party advocates clashed early with the old guard when the Credentials Committee, beset by "sharp factionalism," voted to deny part of McGovern's California delegation on the grounds that the winner-take-all proviso went against the spirit of equality inherent in party reforms.[16] These delegates were crucial, as they meant the difference between a first-ballot nomination and a floor battle. The move, spearheaded by Humphrey's people, infuriated McGovern, who called it "an incredible, cynical, rotten political steal."[17] His forces vowed to take the fight to the floor of the convention and have the delegates reseated. McGovern threatened to bolt the party should an "illegitimate power play" deny him the delegates. In that case, "I would run as an independent or support somebody else on an independent ticket," he said.[18] McGovern supporters on the Credentials Committee struck back against the old guard, challenging Mayor Richard Daley of Chicago and his hand-picked Illinois delegation. The committee voted to deny seats to Daley and his slate on the grounds that they did not meet the goals of racial and gender inclusion set by the reforms. "No one could recall a Democratic leader of comparable power being turned away from a convention with all of his followers," reported the *New York Times*.[19]

Once the convention started, McGovern used old pros such as Pierre Salinger, Abraham Ribicoff, and Senator Fred Harris of Oklahoma to manage a surprisingly strong floor vote over the seating of the California delegation. This victory assured McGovern a first-ballot triumph. The nomination sewn up, his team turned to selecting a running mate. After much debate, the McGovern inner circle settled on Senator Thomas Eagleton of Missouri, putting his name into nomination on Thursday night of convention week. The delegates then proceeded to play political and publicity games with this important task, voting for such figures as newsman Roger Mudd, Chinese leader Mao Tse-tung, and television character Archie Bunker. Voting did not conclude until just after midnight, and McGovern himself did not give his acceptance speech until 2:48 in the morning. Only in Guam was he giving his speech in prime time. An average of 17.8 million households had tuned into the Democratic convention during prime time that week, but when McGovern gave his acceptance speech, the television audience had dropped to 3.6 million homes. In contrast, a month later Richard Nixon would speak to 20.1 million homes during the Republican convention.[20] Few Americans heard McGovern declare:

> From secrecy, and deception in high places, come home, America.
> From a conflict in Indochina which maims our ideals as well as our soldiers, come home, America.
> From military spending so wasteful that it weakens our nation, come home, America.
> From the entrenchment of special privilege and tax favoritism—

From the waste of idle hands to the joy of useful labor—
From the prejudice of race and sex—
From the loneliness of the aging poor and the despair of the
neglected sick, come home, America.
Come home to the affirmation that we have a dream.[21]

The Eagleton Affair

Thomas F. Eagleton, son of a prominent Saint Louis attorney,
a graduate of Amherst College and Harvard Law School, former
attorney general of Missouri, had been a senator since 1968. After
his selection as George McGovern's running mate, the *New York
Times* described him as "urbane and highly personable." The newspaper cited his border-state residence, Catholicism, and relative
youth (he was 42) as bonuses for the ticket. His nearly perfect credentials with organized labor were also listed as beneficial.[22]

The selection of Eagleton had been part of a process that was, at
best, rushed. Distracted by the California problem and the struggle to maintain some semblance of Democratic unity, McGovern
had not put much thought into the vice-presidential selection. Despite the lingering unpleasantness of Chappaquiddick, McGovern
believed that only Ted Kennedy had the name recognition and
standing in the public eye to help his chances of beating Nixon.
While Kennedy gave a series of mixed signals, it never seemed
likely that he would actually take the job, and McGovern turned
to Ribicoff, Senator Walter Mondale of Minnesota, and Senator
Gaylord Nelson of Wisconsin, only to be turned down by each.
McGovern also considered Boston mayor Kevin White but soon
heard rumblings of disapproval from the Massachusetts delegation. White had been a Muskie man in the primary season, and bad
blood evidently still existed within the state. Unwilling to anger
the nominee's home delegation, McGovern resorted to a name
that had been mentioned but not earnestly discussed, Eagleton.[23]

There is some disagreement regarding the mechanics of the
Eagleton selection, but McGovern's former aide Gordon L. Weil
seems to give the most plausible account. As Weil tells it, he was
assigned to do some background checking on possible vice-presidential nominees. A newsman from the *Saint Louis Post-Dispatch*
told the McGovern people that "around Missouri there are strong

rumors of alcoholism or mental illness—or both—in [Eagleton's] background."[24] Everyone on the McGovern team seemed to agree that, if these rumors were true, Eagleton would be dropped. Weil started making phone calls. It appeared that Eagleton did have a weakness for alcohol and had reportedly been hospitalized because of it. Doctors had concluded that Eagleton was not an alcoholic but had a low physiological tolerance for the substance. Weil was assured that Eagleton had no problems in his four years in Washington, but Weil assumed that the mental health problems in Eagleton's "background" referred to someone in the Missourian's family. Democratic activist Anne Wexler apparently tried to warn the McGovern clan about Eagleton's mental-health history, but due to miscommunications the message was never relayed. McGovern offered the job to Eagleton, who quickly accepted. Asked if he had any "skeletons" in his closet the campaign should know about, Eagleton flatly said, "no."[25]

The week following the convention, McGovern retired to Custer State Park in South Dakota for some time away from the campaign grind. It was there that he first became aware of reports of serious mental illness in Eagleton's past. The candidate learned that the Knight-Ridder wire service was set to report that Eagleton had been hospitalized three times in the 1960s with mental exhaustion and depression. On two occasions, Eagleton had received shock therapy. Eagleton was flown to South Dakota to see McGovern, and a hasty press conference was arranged in which Eagleton told all to the media. "You have seen here today," McGovern said, "a demonstration of the candor and openness you're going to get from Senator Eagleton and me. We have no secrets. We have nothing to hide."[26] He claimed that even if he had known of Eagleton's past it would have changed nothing. He was convinced that Tom Eagleton was prepared "in mind, body and spirit" to be vice-president or president.[27] The next day, McGovern proclaimed, "I am 1,000 per cent for Tom Eagleton and have no intention of dropping him from the ticket."[28]

McGovern's handling of the Eagleton affair would doom his candidacy. Soon after he declared himself squarely in Eagleton's corner, opinion polls suggested that Eagleton was dead weight on the ticket. A *Newsweek* poll indicated that 17 percent of Democrats and 33 percent of independents were feeling "less friendly" towards the McGovern candidacy because of Eagleton's past illnesses.[29] As time progressed, it became clear that the subject of Eagleton's competency had immobilized the campaign. Major newspapers, including the *Washington Post* and *New York Times*, editorialized that Eagleton should step down. Belying his own 1000-percent support statement, McGovern tried to send signals through the press that Eagleton should bow out on his own. Often "sources close to McGovern" were McGovern himself. The candidate now suggested that he would listen to the people on the issue. With Eagleton away on a campaign swing, McGovern stated, "I'm with Senator Eagleton all the way—until he and I have a chance to talk."[30] Fund raising at a halt and a majority of his staff in favor of dumping Eagleton, McGovern finally bowed to pressure. In a meeting in Washington, Eagleton agreed to leave the ticket on 31 July 1972.[31]

Once again, McGovern had to select a running mate. After Kennedy turned him down a second time, McGovern was also spurned by Ribicoff, Humphrey, Florida governor Ruben Askew, and Muskie. Finally, McGovern received a positive reaction from Kennedy-clan-member Sargent Shriver. Upon his selection, Shriver quipped: "I am not embarrassed to be George McGovern's seventh choice for Vice President [a slight exaggeration]. We Democrats may be short of money; we're not short of talent. Pity Mr. Nixon—his first and only choice was Spiro Agnew."[32] Married to a Kennedy sister, Shriver gave McGovern the Kennedy cachet if not the Kennedy name. The former head of the Chicago Merchandise Mart, head of the Peace Corps, and ambassador to France, Shriver was certainly a credible replacement for Eagleton. But the damage had been done. A Harris poll had McGovern down to a 34-percent rating following the Eagleton mess.[33]

Some of the blame for the Eagleton affair should probably go to McGovern's staff for not having the foresight to investigate the short list of vice-presidential candidates thoroughly before and during the convention. Surely, most of the blame must land on Eagleton himself, who declared in an interview that he did not see his past emotional problems as skeletons in his closet. "Skeletons are things where you have committed a crime," he stated, "where you have stolen from clients or violated legal ethics or something sinister like that."[34] It certainly was unwise of Eagleton to think that the information about his past would not come to light or would not hurt the ticket. Perhaps in his eagerness for the vice-presidential nomination, Eagleton's judgment failed him. Some of the blame for the repercussions of the debacle must go to McGovern himself. Staking his electoral claim on his dedication to truth and forthrightness in politics, McGovern let down those principles by publicly supporting Eagleton and then later under-mining him in private. McGovern's early statements regarding Eagleton were imprudent. Thus, when it became clear that Eagleton's candidacy could not be sustained, McGovern was forced to contradict his principles, an act that seemed like duplicity to much of the public. The Eagleton affair permanently labeled the Mc-Govern campaign as sloppy and unprofessional and the top of the ticket as unprepared to be president of the United States.[35]

The Candidates Take Stands

Normally, a presidential candidate receives a "bounce" from his nominating convention. The chaos of the Democratic convention, coupled with the Eagleton imbroglio, contributed to McGovern's actually slipping farther behind President Nixon in the polls. The senator was still having problems holding the traditional Demo-cratic coalition together, much less reaching out to the indepen-dents and Republicans, both of whom he would need to win the office. As the *New York Times* put it during the convention, "The Democrats have dramatized . . . not only that they are not united, but also that they are deeply divided on policy, on tactics, and on the priorities before the nation."[36] McGovern campaign manager Larry O'Brien later noted that the period between the Democratic convention and election day were the "three worst months of my life."[37]

Nowhere was the division more apparent than with organized labor. As McGovern's formal nomination approached, one spokes-man for organized labor greeted it "with bitterness, obscenities and a threat to withhold campaign funds."[38] I. W. Abel, head of United Steelworkers, declared, "there are no reasons" to support the Democratic ticket.[39] The biggest blow came when George

Meany, who sharply disagreed with McGovern's Vietnam proposals, announced that the AFL-CIO would offer no endorsement in
the presidential race. While local unions were free to do as they
pleased, this statement from headquarters certainly sent a signal
to all organized labor that McGovern was not someone to be en-
thused about. It also robbed McGovern of the money that the AFL-
CIO would normally have spent mobilizing Democratic voters.
Salt was poured on the wound when, shortly thereafter, Meany
was seen golfing with Richard Nixon. This amounted to a tacit endorsement by Meany, which went along with the outright endorsement of Nixon by the Teamsters.[40] McGovern insisted that he
could win without the support of labor or Richard Daley's Chicago
machine. Daley himself announced that he supported the whole
Democratic ticket, "federal, state and local," but could not bring
himself to mention McGovern by name.[41] One of Daley's hand-
picked Illinois candidates said, "I let these national leaders take
care of themselves. We concentrate on our own local people."[42]
McGovern hoped to gain new voters, especially among the newly
enfranchised young, who could make up for the loss of some of
the labor vote.

The Nixon people themselves seemed to have a campaign plan
that consisted of no campaigning. Aides to Nixon urged the president to limit himself to a three-week effort rather than the traditional two-month campaign starting on Labor Day.[43] Most Nixon
campaigning would be done through surrogates such as George
Shultz, Barry Goldwater, Senator Robert Dole, and young congressman Jack Kemp. In fact, Nixon was described as "the least
accessible Presidential candidate of modern times."[44] McGovern
tried to goad Nixon into debates. "The American people are entitled," the Democrat said, "to have the two candidates submit to
rigorous probing by each other on the direction the country is to
choose for the next four years."[45] Nixon demurred. "When we are
involved in a war," he argued, "for a President in the heat of partisan debate to make policy would not be in the national interest."[46]

Nixon did court traditional Democratic voters. Former treasury
secretary John Connally formed a group called "Democrats for
Nixon." The president verbally opposed abortion and school busing, while supporting aid to parochial schools in an attempt to win

over Catholic and ethnic voters. One of his few campaign stops would be at the Statue of Liberty to make a speech praising immigration. He also targeted the 147 electoral votes of the South, hoping to create "a new era of political alignment" in that region.[47] Nixon mostly ran on vague notions of holding the line on taxes and "the work ethic" in opposition to what he called McGovern's "welfare ethic."[48] All in all, the Nixon people were confident in their man's chances of beating McGovern. White House political advisor Harry Dent had declared before the Democratic convention, "Some people around here are about to wee-wee in their pants waiting for [McGovern] to get the nomination."[49]

It was on defense policy and the war in Vietnam that McGovern and Nixon diverged most profoundly. In 1968, candidate Nixon had stated, "Those who have had a chance for four years and could not produce peace should not be given another chance."[50] President Nixon admitted that he had broken this campaign promise but argued that McGovern would have peace "at the cost of surrender, dishonor and the destruction of the U.S. ability to conduct foreign policy in a responsible way."[51] McGovern, on the other hand, favored a unilateral, rather than negotiated, withdrawal from Vietnam. He contended, "Mr. Nixon has kept the war going for four years and ground up 20,000 American lives 'purely to avoid criticism of the right-wing war hawks.'"[52] McGovern called for the ending of bombing and acts of war and a withdrawal of all United States forces and equipment. He proposed sending Shriver to Hanoi to negotiate the return of POWs and allowing the Vietnamese to work out their own settlement. In addition, McGovern advocated amnesty for most who had avoided the draft through illegal means and increased benefits for veterans.[53] In his nomination acceptance speech, McGovern made the promise, "Within ninety days of my inauguration, every American soldier and every American prisoner will be out of the jungle and out of their cells and back home in America where they belong."[54]

McGovern's positions on national defense policy mirrored his position on the war. In an attempt to promote his other objectives, McGovern took a broad view of American foreign-policy interests. "National security includes schools for our children as well as silos for our missiles, the health of our families as much as the size of our bombs, the safety of our streets and the condition of our cities and not just the engines of war." McGovern told the Democratic National Committee, "Let us have smarter children instead of smarter bombs." On another occasion, he claimed that America had become "obsessed with the fear of 'international Communism,'" which led it to waste money on weapons systems such as the "elaborate F-15 aircraft."[55] Under a McGovern administration, he promised, the United States military would see greatly reduced numbers of nuclear warheads, aircraft carriers, and strategic bombers. The proposed Nixon defense budget for 1973 called for over $80 billion in spending. In contrast, McGovern projected spending of only $54.8 billion by 1975.[56] This projection led Nixon to accuse McGovern of "gamb[ling] with the safety of the American people under a false banner of economy."[57]

The differences in their economic programs may not have been as severe as in defense policy, but Nixon and McGovern still differed widely on how best to help America prosper. *Time* characterized McGovern's economic program as "more like the mixed economies and relatively paternalistic societies of Western Europe." Both candidates supported some form of guaranteed income, but McGovern was far more generous in his proposals, advocating a one-thousand-dollar guaranteed income for all Americans to be paid from hikes in individual and corporate income taxes and inheritance taxes.[58] He also sought to guarantee jobs for all Americans. "Whatever employment the private sector does not provide," he said, "the federal government will either stimulate, or provide itself."[59] The Democratic candidate championed dramatic increases in federal spending on education and universal health-care coverage and advocated $44 billion in new spending on such items as public transportation, agricultural subsidies, and drug-control programs. The increase was to be paid for by cutting defense and closing tax loopholes.[60] In an early September speech on Wall Street, McGovern stated, "Free enterprise and social responsibility . . . must coexist side by side."[61]

McGovern's economic policy proposals certainly hurt him among the business class. *Newsweek* reported, "With few exceptions, businessmen have found his tax-reform ideas confiscatory, his welfare and budget ideas inflationary." In what must have sounded almost like a compliment, the writer asserted that Mc-Govern "inspired more open hostility [on Wall Street] than any Democratic nominee since Franklin Delano Roosevelt."[62] Indeed, the *New York Times* even suggested that just the prospect of a Mc-Govern candidacy was "widely believed to have been one factor in the stock market's recent weakness."[63] Unfortunately for McGov-ern, however, economic conditions had seldom looked better. In-flation had slowed, and in the second quarter of 1972, the economy grew at an almost unheard of annual rate of 8.9 percent.[64] *News-week* reported, "Businessmen, bankers and economists alike [are] in a rarely unanimous glow of approval for the state of the econ-omy."[65] They were not likely to support a radical new economic model.

The lack of support in the economic community was mirrored in the general public. A poll in late August had McGovern down by a two-to-one margin in sixteen key states. Ominously, the poll predicted that McGovern would gain less than half the Democratic voters. Nixon was holding leads among core Democratic constitu-encies such as union members.[66] Some polls presented a picture that in hindsight seems incredible. A *Time* poll released in Octo-ber showed 55 percent of the public identifying Nixon as the "peace candidate," with only 30 percent giving McGovern the designa-tion. The same poll had voters identifying Nixon as more likely to run an "open and trustworthy" administration.[67] A *Newsweek* poll in late August had already indicated that Nixon solidly out-paced McGovern among the public on such qualities as "logical and clear thinker," "listens to what others say," and, most surpris-ingly, "earnest and sincere." Twenty-four percent identified Nixon as a moderate, while only 9 percent said the same of McGovern. Conversely, 20 percent thought McGovern matched the descrip-tion of "extremist," while only 3 percent put the label on Nixon.[68]

This poll was released only weeks after a group of men had been arrested breaking into the Democratic National Committee offices at the Watergate Hotel in Washington, D.C. The scandal that would ultimately bring down the presidency of Richard Nixon was only in its infancy. Still, McGovern's last attempt to gain traction with the American people concerned the corruption of the Nixon White House. He tagged the president as leader of "the most morally corrupt Administration in the history of the United States."[69] Late in the campaign, he charged, "Nixon is up to his ears in political sabotage. He has got to take responsibility for it."[70] On the Watergate break-in, Sargent Shriver declared, "If he knew this was going on, President Nixon is guilty of immoral and illegal acts."[71] "The President," McGovern argued, "sets the moral tone of the nation, and this Administration reeks with permissiveness toward . . . corrupt interests."[72] On national television, the Democrat charged Nixon with bringing the nation to "a moral and a constitutional crisis of unprecedented dimensions." He laid "the whole ugly mess of corruption, of sabotage, of wire-tapping right squarely in the lap of Richard Nixon."[73] McGovern had also speculated out loud that Nixon was "at least indirectly" responsible for Watergate, which was "the kind of thing you expect under a person like Hitler."[74] While the first part of the statement was reasonable at the time and, of course, more than true in retrospect, the Hitler reference produced strong denouncements of McGovern in the press.

On none of these issues could the Democrats gain traction. On election night—7 November 1972—George McGovern experienced one of the worst defeats in American presidential-election history. Nixon took forty-nine of fifty states, including McGovern's home state of South Dakota. The Republican candidate won 60.7 percent of the popular vote to the Democrat's 37.5 percent. McGovern managed victories only in Massachusetts and the District of Columbia.[75] He had scored an amazing political upset in winning the Democratic nomination, but the grassroots were not fertile enough to bring McGovern to victory in November.

Conclusion

What led to such a spectacular defeat? First, it must be said that removing an incumbent president is quite difficult. The opponent has to give the public a compelling reason for replacing a sitting president. This task is formidable under the most favorable circumstances, and McGovern did not have favorable circumstances. As stated above, the economic outlook in the summer and autumn

Days before the 1972 election, Democratic presidential candidate George McGovern and wife Eleanor boarded the Dakota Queen II after campaigning in Corpus Cristi, Texas. Photograph by Dennis Warren

of 1972 was positive. On the war, even though one-third of American combat deaths in Vietnam occurred under Richard Nixon, the president paradoxically benefited in 1972 from the decline in draft calls and casualties from previous highs. People perceived that Nixon was winding down the war and accepted the premise that America could not just pack up and leave Vietnam but must do so "honorably." McGovern's moralism on the issue was hard for many to swallow, suggesting as it did that the American effort was worthless.[76]

Rightly or wrongly, too many voters saw McGovern as an extremist. The wisdom of the time suggested that America was not ready for many of McGovern's policy proposals. Republican strategist Kevin P. Phillips, famous for his book *The Emerging Republican Majority*, argued, "McGovern represents a new radical elite that has taken control of the Democratic Party and alienated much of the traditional party structure in the process."[77] Political analysts Richard Scammon and Ben J. Wattenberg pointed out that the middle is "where victory lies. The great majority of the voters of America are unyoung, unpoor and unblack."[78] McGovern's campaign director Frank Mankiewicz stated: "We reacted to every threat from women, or militants, or college groups. If I had to do it all over again, I'd learn when to tell them to go to hell."[79] The nation decided early that it wanted to reelect Richard Nixon, and there was little McGovern could do to persuade voters otherwise. McGovern's own conclusion was that Nixon would have been tough to beat under good conditions, but that the Eagleton confusion put the election into landslide territory.[80] The pandemonium of the convention and the unfortunate public squabbles among the candidate's staff, over which McGovern had little or no control, added to an overall aura of chaos within the campaign that doomed his candidacy.

The 1972 election also represented the splintering of the old New Deal coalition. While Republicans would never quite succeed in turning this fissure into a permanent majority of their own, the Democrats' ownership of the votes of blue-collar workers, Catholics, and urban ethnics ended in the 1972 election. It might be said that the "Reagan Democrat" first appeared in helping to elect Richard Nixon eight years before Reagan's own success. In later years, the Democratic party also determined that their ultra-democratic nomination reforms were flawed. To correct the problem, they subsequently introduced the "super-delegate" as a way of guaranteeing representation of Democratic officeholders and party regulars at the convention.[81]

George McGovern's run at the White House had lasting impact in two areas. First, the South Dakota Democrat was a prophet in his quest against corruption in politics. He promoted and practiced many campaign reforms that now are standard law, such as public disclosure of campaign contributions. He was clearly right about the depths of corruption in the Nixon White House. While McGovern may have been trolling for votes in making his accusation, it still does not change the fact that he was correct. Had the election been held one year later, with far more information in the public's hands, the outcome may have been different. In one of the more prescient statements of the election, writer Stewart Alsop declared in September that Nixon had been lucky in his reelection campaign, from Chappaquiddick to Eagleton, but "at some time in the next four years, if he is re-elected, Mr. Nixon's run of luck seems likely to run out."[82]

Lastly, many of those party regulars who would take super-delegate slots in the 1980s and 1990s cut their teeth in the 1972 campaign. Gary Hart and Bill Clinton are two obvious examples of individuals who received their first taste of presidential politics by serving George McGovern. The "McGovernites," as they are sometimes called, became the heart and soul of the Democratic party. While clashes still occur between the more moderate "electable wing" (to use their term) and the McGovernite wing of the Democratic party, there can be no doubt that the senator provided a great service in introducing so many Americans to the world of political activism and public service. For this reason alone, the Democratic party and the nation owe George McGovern a debt of gratitude.

NOTES

1. McGovern, *Grassroots: The Autobiography of George McGovern* (New York: Random House, 1977), p. 159. *See also* Robert Sam Anson, *McGovern: A Biography* (New York: Holt, Reinhart & Winston, 1972), p. 260.

2. McGovern, *Grassroots*, pp. 152–53.

3. McGovern, *An American Journey: The Presidential Campaign Speeches of George McGovern* (New York: Random House, 1974), pp. 5–6.

4. "Nixon: Determined to Make a Difference," *Time*, 3 Jan. 1972, p. 10.

5. "Will the Democrats Nominate Muskie?," *Time*, 7 Feb. 1972, p. 24.

6. "Supplement: A Preview of the Primaries," *Time*, 6 Mar. 1972, unpaged.

7. "Muskie Wins, M'Govern 2d in New Hampshire Voting," *New York Times*, 8 Mar. 1972, p. 1.

8. Ibid., p. 26.

9. Quoted in "Supplement: A Preview of the Primaries."

10. Theodore H. White, *The Making of the President, 1972* (New York: Atheneum Publishers, 1973), p. 96.

11. "M'Govern Winner in Wisconsin," *New York Times*, 5 Apr. 1972, p. 1.

12. "The McGovern Issue," *Time*, 22 May 1972, p. 19. Of course, these charges were exaggerations at best. McGovern's 1972 position on abortion was no different than Justice Antonin Scalia's today. While McGovern felt that abortion should be a woman's choice, he believed as a matter of law that it should be left to the states. McGovern was for the decriminalization of most marijuana-possession charges. As McGovern pointed out, his position on amnesty for resisters had a long tradition in American wars. *See also* "McGovern Moves Front, Maybe Center," *Time*, 19 June 1972, p. 15.

13. "The Big Showdown in California," *Time*, 5 June 1972, p. 21; "McGovern Moves Front, Maybe Center," pp. 13–14.

14. "A Setback for McGovern," *Time*, 10 July 1972, p. 15.

15. White, *Making of the President, 1972*, p. 179. For more on the new rules, *see* Chapter 6, by Stephen K. Ward.

16. "Democrats Move for Conciliation in Seating Rifts," *New York Times*, 2 July 1972, p. 1.

17. Quoted in "Can They Stop McGovern?," *Newsweek*, 10 July 1972, p. 16.

18. Quoted in "McGovern Said to Plan to Bolt if He Is Rebuffed," *New York Times*, 2 July 1972, p. 28.

19. "Panel Denies Convention Seats to 59 Daley Delegates," *New York Times*, 1 July 1972, p. 1. *See also* "Can They Stop McGovern?," pp. 16–17.

20. White, *Making of the President, 1972*, pp. 184–86, 244.

21. McGovern, *American Journey*, p. 23.

22. "M'Govern Names Eagleton Running Mate," *New York Times*, 14 July 1972, pp. 1, 11. *See also* "Missouri's Contribution to the Ticket," ibid., p. 10.

23. McGovern, *Grassroots*, pp. 196–98.

24. Quoted in Weil, *The Long Shot: George McGovern Runs for President* (New York: W. W. Norton & Co., 1973), pp. 162–63.

25. Ibid., pp. 164–65, 168–69. *See also* Gary Warren Hart, *Right from the Start: A Chronicle of the McGovern Campaign* (New York: Quadrangle, 1973), pp. 239–40.

26. Quoted in "Eagleton Tells of Shock Therapy on Two Occasions," *New York Times*, 26 July 1972, pp. 1, 20.

27. "Excerpts from Eagleton News Parley," ibid., p. 20.

28. Quoted in "M'Govern Urged by Some Backers to Drop Eagleton," ibid., 27 July 1972, p. 1.

29. "A Crisis Named Eagleton," *Newsweek*, 7 Aug. 1972, p. 12.

30. "McGovern's First Crisis: The Eagleton Affair," *Time*, 7 Aug. 1972, pp. 11, 13.

31. Weil, *Long Shot*, p. 180.

32. Quoted in "The Democrats Begin Again," *Time*, 21 Aug. 1972, p. 10.

33. Ibid., p. 11.

34. Quoted in "'Self, It Won't Be Easy,'" *Newsweek*, 7 Aug. 1972, p. 19.

35. McGovern himself reached many of these same conclusions in his autobiography, *Grassroots*, pp. 207–16.

36. James Reston, "McGovern Victory: New Tasks," *New York Times*, 12 July 1972, p. 18.

37. Quoted in Melvin Small, *The Presidency of Richard Nixon* (Lawrence: University Press of Kansas, 1999), p. 259.

38. Quoted in Ben A. Franklin, "McGovern's Gain Embitters Labor," *New York Times*, 12 July 1972, p. 20.

39. Quoted in "M'Govern Names Eagleton Running Mate," *New York Times*, 14 July 1972, p. 11.

40. "Labor Decides to Mugwump It," *Time*, 31 July 1972, pp. 13–14; Weil, *Long Shot*, pp. 152–55.

41. Quoted in "Fitful Pause for McGovern," *Time*, 31 July 1972, p. 14. Daley would later campaign with McGovern, but it was always clear that the mayor's support was less than full-hearted.

42. Edward Hanrahan, quoted in "Daley Si, McGovern No," *Newsweek*, 7 Aug. 1972, p. 9.

43. "O'Brien Criticizes Connally Tactics," *New York Times*, 22 July 1972, p. 11.

44. "The Hard-to-Cover Campaign," *Newsweek*, 23 Oct. 1972, p. 118.

45. Quoted in "M'Govern Seeking Nixon TV Debates," *New York Times*, 23 July 1972, p. 1.

46. Quoted in "Republicans: The Presidential Hat," *Newsweek*, 11 Sept. 1972, p. 21.

47. Quoted in "The South Rises Again—for Nixon," ibid., 23 Oct. 1972, p. 37.

48. Quoted in "Some Political Sparks But Still No Fire," *Time*, 18 Sept. 1972, p. 16.

49. Quoted in "Advantage to the Incumbent," ibid., 10 July 1972, p. 17.

50. Quoted in "McGovern v. Nixon on the War," ibid., 23 Oct. 1972, p. 33.

51. Quoted in "Richard Nixon's Three Hats," ibid., 11 Sept. 1972, pp. 16, 18.

52. Quoted in "The Devil and George McGovern," *Newsweek*, 6 Nov. 1972, p. 136. This argument was difficult to sustain as Nixon's policy of détente, which included going to China and the Soviet Union and negotiating the SALT agreement, was largely denounced by the anti-Communist right wing. Nixon did not seem shy about shocking the sensibilities of the hawks in these areas.

53. "Peace, Politics—and Great Expectations," *Newsweek*, 23 Oct. 1972, p. 33.

54. McGovern, *American Journey*, p. 20.

55. Ibid., pp. 21, 28, 92, 94.

56. "A Little Protective Reaction," *Time*, 19 June 1972, p. 17; McGovern, *American Journey*, p. 85.

57. "A New Majority for Four More Years?," *Time*, 4 Sept. 1972, p. 15.

58. "Front and Center for George McGovern," ibid., 8 May 1972, p. 19.

59. McGovern, *American Journey*, p. 22.

60. "Front and Center for George McGovern," *Time*, 8 May 1972, pp. 19–20; "McGovernomics: A More Modest Proposal," ibid., 11 Sept. 1972, pp. 14–15.

61. Quoted in "The Beginning of the Beginning?," *Newsweek*, 11 Sept. 1972, p. 18.

62. "McGovern through a Loophole Darkly," ibid., p. 53.

63. Terry Robards, "M'Govern Views Alarm Big Donors on Wall Street," *New York Times*, 3 July 1972, p. 1.

64. "Gain in Economy Fastest since '65; Price Rise Slows," *New York Times*, 22 July 1972, p. 1.

65. "Mr. Nixon 'Told You So,'" *Newsweek*, 21 Aug. 1972, p. 65.

66. "In 16 Key States, Nixon Leads 2 to 1," *Time*, 28 Aug. 1972, pp.

15–16; "Who Speaks for the Union Voter?," *Newsweek*, 18 Sept. 1972, p. 21.

67. "Nixon Moves Out to an Astonishing Lead," *Time*, 2 Oct. 1972, pp. 13–14.

68. "What America Really Thinks of Nixon," *Newsweek*, 28 Aug. 1972, pp. 16–18.

69. Quoted in "McGovern Tries Giving 'em Hell," *Newsweek*, 16 Oct. 1972, p. 29.

70. Quoted in "Denials and Still More Questions," *Time*, 30 Oct. 1972, p. 19.

71. Quoted in "The Hard-Luck Crusade," *Time*, 6 Nov. 1972, p. 44.

72. Quoted in "McGovern Tries Giving 'em Hell," *Newsweek*, 16 Oct. 1972, p. 29.

73. Quoted in "The Look of a Landslide," *Newsweek*, 6 Nov. 1972, p. 41.

74. Quoted in "American Notes: The Hitler Analogy," *Time*, 28 Aug. 1972, p. 8.

75. White, *Making of the President, 1972*, pp. 342, 372–73.

76. "McGovern v. Nixon on the War," *Time*, 23 Oct. 1972, pp. 34–35.

77. Quoted in "The Confrontation of the Two Americas," *Time*, 2 Oct. 1972, p. 16.

78. Quoted in "McGovern Moves Front, Maybe Center," *Time*, 19 June 1972, p. 13.

79. Quoted in White, *Making of the President, 1972*, p. 44.

80. McGovern, *Grassroots*, p. 191.

81. Super-delegates are senators, governors, congressmen, and other distinguished party leaders.

82. Alsop, "A Conversation with Nixon aboard Air Force One," *Newsweek*, 4 Sept. 1972, p. 26.

CHAPTER EIGHT

AMBASSADOR McGOVERN,

ELDER STATESMAN

RUSSELL E. WILLIS

 *I've been around a long time and I've made my share of mistakes as well as things that were worthwhile. And I do think there's something to be said for the wisdom that comes simply with living a long time. So I consider it a proud compliment when people refer to me as an elder statesman.*[1] *— George McGovern, 11 Sept. 2003*

George McGovern has played many roles in a life that spans eight decades and counting, among them: child of the prairie, decorated warrior, husband and father, professor, grassroots politician, White House bureaucrat, United States congressman and senator, leader of the loyal opposition to the Vietnam War, presidential candidate, writer, social commentator, activist against substance abuse, and businessman. From the Great Depression to the end of the Cold War, McGovern was both a product of this remarkable century as well as one of its movers and shakers. Yet, by the mid-1990s, as he entered his mid-seventies, he seemed fated to follow the twentieth century into the history books. But just before the century had exhausted its tremendous energies, he burst back into the national and international consciousness bearing the title ambassador and leading the world to embark on the task of eliminating hunger in a generation. As Ambassador McGovern, he added to his impressive résumé the title of "elder statesman." His voice now commanded the respect reserved for those considered wise, not just powerful or merely intelligent. His leadership was now grounded, not on the authority of law or power of government, but on the basis of lifelong achievement and time-tested character.

A Job Description

For it to carry any real value, the expression "elder statesman" or "elder stateswoman" cannot simply refer to politicians or government officials who have lived long lives. Neither can it stand for old people who used to be politicians or government officials. Rather, it implies both a quality and quantity of accomplishment, service to the state (and to the greater good), historical significance, efficacy, wisdom, and recognition that leads such persons to be heeded when they speak and followed where they lead. Being an elder in this sense means both the sheer number of years of life experience as well as the fact that the person is seen as one who has stood up well under the weight of those years. It is probably not accidental that most of the individuals upon whose shoulders are laid the mantle of elder statesperson are those who have achieved through adversity, not simply those who have achieved.[2]

The title of elder statesperson is honorific in the most profound sense. He or she may carry some sort of official standing or authority in a government, political party, or other public institution. However, the capacity of such individuals to affect public opinion and persuade others to act for the greater good transcends bureaucratic authority and rests, rather, with their place in the social consciousness.[3] Further, though the title itself refers to service to the "state," historically this citation has been reserved for those whose service is free from partisan politics and places the good of the nation within the context of a commitment to civilization and peaceful coexistence grounded in justice rather than narrowly defined national self-interest. Even, and especially, in times of war, the elder statesperson's support or criticism of a specific nation's interests is grounded in the transcendent goals of justice, sustainable peace, and prosperity.

While proudly wearing the title elder statesman, George McGovern balks at the notion of himself as old or "retired." In 2003, having just celebrated his eighty-first birthday, McGovern kept a schedule of speaking engagements and events linked to his humanitarian pursuits that would bring most of us to our knees. On the second anniversary of the 11 September 2001 terrorist attacks, and soon after his birthday, McGovern reflected on life as he entered his eighty-second year: "I think if we fully retire in the sense that [is] sometimes used, it means just doing nothing, sitting around and twiddling our thumbs. I think that's when death begins. . . . As long as you're active and caring and working and doing, I think you're basically young. I don't feel any older today than I did when I ran for president at the age of forty-nine. I'm eighty-one now, but I can honestly say my spirit is as young as it was at forty-nine when I was trying to get elected president."[4]

McGovern's modest acceptance of his status as an elder statesman is also a product of his self-image. Various biographies and personal memoirs published over the last three decades document his personal reserve, even humility, in the face of both his authority and responsibility as a national and international leader. For instance, in recognition of McGovern's service as president of the Middle East Policy Council, Howard Campbell, chairman of the American Business Council of the Gulf Countries, thanked him for his "unique blend of humility, insightfulness, and probity."[5]

McGovern is no shrinking violet, however. Robert Sam Anson, his first biographer, referred to him as a "deceptively self-assured and even prideful man," going on to chronicle many contests of will in which McGovern was caught up before and during his 1972 presidential campaign—some of which he won and others, notably the presidential campaign itself, that he lost.[6] McGovern's passion and determination are clear to all who meet him. But these qualities are muted by conscience and the desire to be the messenger and not the message. He exemplifies the humble assurance of one who has learned that if you are doing good, you do not have to prove yourself—to be good is good enough.

When faced, for example, with attacks on his personal courage and patriotism during the Vietnam War, he did not use his World War II experiences and accomplishments, including the fact that he was a decorated hero, as a defense against his political detractors. Many have speculated in recent years whether modesty and his naturally quiet and introspective demeanor harmed his presidential aspirations.[7] In a 2001 interview of Stephen Ambrose following publication of his book *The Wild Blue* about McGovern and his B-24 crewmates, the author was asked why McGovern was "reluctant to trumpet his war record during the campaign." Ambrose responded: "None of the press people ever seemed to be interested in bringing it up—nobody ever asked him about it, to my recollection. There are millions of veterans out there that this same thing is true of. They're not so much reluctant to recall what they experienced, but they are not going to volunteer anything if no one asks. In George's case, I just think that he felt the time had come to share his story."[8] As in the words of Ecclesiastes, "to everything there is a season." By the early years of the twenty-first century, McGovern was one of the last of his generation, one of the last who *could* tell this story. So he did, with no glorification but in the quiet voice of an elder, one who could speak with authority about sacrifice and service.

Elder Statesman in Waiting, 1981–1998

McGovern faded from the political limelight following his departure from the Senate in 1981. He returned briefly to challenge Ronald Reagan and the New Right by seeking the Democratic presidential nomination in 1984.[9] Although he withdrew from the race and never again ran for political office, he certainly did not put himself out to pasture. In addition to trying his hand at business, McGovern filled his time with three primary pursuits that focused his energies during the decade from 1984 to 1994.

The first pursuit was actually a return to the profession he had forsaken for politics—that of college professor. As the quintessential "antiwarrior" of the Vietnam era, a true grassroots populist, and victim of the Watergate conspiracy, McGovern appeared for lectures, conferences, workshops, and rallies on hundreds of campuses. But as the 1980s waned and the world spun out of the Cold War era, McGovern was increasingly viewed, especially by intellectuals and academics, as one of the architects of late-twentieth-century politics and culture. As such, he found himself courted by some of the most prestigious universities in the United States and abroad. His résumé came to include visiting professorships at institutions like Columbia University, the University of Pennsylvania, Northwestern University, Duke University, the University of New Orleans, Cornell University, American University, George Washington University, the University of Innsbruck, Munich University, and the University of Berlin.[10]

After retiring from the Senate, McGovern
taught at universities, wrote, and worked as
an ambassador for the United Nations.
He is pictured here in September 1990 at
age 68.

His second pursuit was writing. Prior to 1984, he had published five books: *War against Want* (1964), *Agricultural Thought in the Twentieth Century* (1967), *A Time of War, a Time of Peace* (1968), *The Great Coalfield War* (1972), and his autobiography, *Grassroots* (1977). In the early 1990s, McGovern continued writing in the area of his political fame and infamy—the Vietnam War and politics. He served as a contributor to *Vietnam: Four American Perspectives* (1990) and wrote the foreword to *Give Peace a Chance: Exploring the Vietnam Antiwar Movement* (1992), a collection of essays presented at the Vietnam Antiwar Movement Conference held in Toledo, Ohio, in May 1990 and dedicated to the memory of historian Charles DeBenedetti.

During the 1990s, McGovern began to concentrate on the two issues that would dominate his work at the turn of the twenty-first century—hunger and liberalism. In 1992, he contributed to *Food and Population: The World in Crisis.* This work reflected his enduring concern for the hungry, which had been a centerpiece of his earlier political career as director of the Office of Food for Peace in the Kennedy Administration and in the development of America's school-lunch, food-stamp, and Women, Infants, and Children (WIC) programs, which were set up during the 1960s and 1970s through bipartisan collaboration with Republican Senator Robert Dole. Also in 1992, McGovern contributed to David P. Barash's *The L Word: An Unapologetic, Thoroughly Biased, Long-Overdue Explication and Celebration of Liberalism.* His passionate defense of liberalism in the face of Ronald Reagan's conservative revolution (and its lingering shadow in the first Bush Administration and the Republican Congresses of the Clinton years) would continue into the new millennium during the presidency of George W. Bush.

McGovern's third pursuit was helping to bridge two cultures—those of America and the Middle East—whose destinies had become interlaced through the multibillion-dollar economics of oil, the politics of terrorism, and the seemingly unending cycle of war that created ever-changing patterns of friend and foe. For his part, McGovern served through most of the 1990s as president of the Middle East Policy Council (MEPC), created in 1981 to pro-

mote understanding of Middle Eastern cultures, politics, and economics through educational programs and cooperative ventures.
As MEPC president, McGovern continued to hone the skills of
multilateral negotiation and nonpartisan politics that had served
him well in his earlier political life and to hold his finger to the
pulse of the post-Cold War era.[11]

As the 1990s wore on, McGovern entered what could have been
a quiet, relatively productive, but generally unremarkable twilight
to his career and life. In mid-decade, however, two events occurred that would shake his world. On 13 December 1994, George
and Eleanor McGovern learned of the death of their beloved but
troubled daughter Teresa. Terry's death after years of struggling
with substance abuse lit a fire in George's soul. In 1996, he published *Terry: My Daughter's Life-and-Death Struggle with Alcoholism*,
a personal account of a parent's love, helplessness, and struggle
for understanding in the face of addiction's grip on his child. In
the same year, George and Eleanor created the McGovern Family
Foundation to fund research, treatment, and support of individuals and families affected by alcoholism. George threw himself into
this cause and traveled throughout the country, telling the McGoverns' story and aiding efforts to combat substance abuse and bol-
ster the social safety net for those with psychological problems.
As he did so, he experienced a renewed commitment to those in
need.

The second momentous event that changed McGovern's fate
was his appointment by President William Clinton in 1997 to be
the United States ambassador to the United Nations Food and
Agriculture Organization in Rome. This appointment was, no
doubt, a means for Clinton (who cut his political teeth during Mc-
Govern's 1972 presidential campaign) to show respect for his political mentor and friend. But it was also a way for the president to
harness the passions of the elder statesman. Since the days when
the decorated B-24 pilot had flown food to starving Europeans immediately following World War II, McGovern had dedicated much
of his public service to addressing the scourge of hunger. In a
stroke of historical coincidence, the seventy-five-year-old ambassador returned to Italy, the country from which he had launched
both his combat and humanitarian missions almost half a century

before, to work with the World Food Programme (WFP), an organization that he had helped to establish as a young member of the
Kennedy White House. Thus, with his ambassadorial credential
in hand, McGovern resigned from the Middle East Policy Council presidency effective 30 November 1997, and he and Eleanor
prepared to move to Rome.[12]

Elder Statesman "with Credential"

Arriving in Rome in 1998, the newly minted ambassador must
have felt exhilarated at the opportunity for a new start, even at this
late age, to pursue a life dream, as well as the resources to ful-
fill that dream. In this case, his resources were substantial. First,
George McGovern was a duly appointed ambassador representing
the most powerful and wealthy nation on earth. Second, he was
working with what was, arguably, the most effective organization
in the world for combating hunger. Third, he came to the job with
a lifelong passion and life experiences that would motivate and
equip him for this work. Fourth, not only did he have name recognition and know how to use it, his notability was bolstered by
the fact that he was becoming widely accepted as an elder statesman by his American colleagues, by foreign diplomats and politicians, by aid-agency personnel, by the popular press, and even by
his bosses back in Washington, D.C.[13] Fifth, he had the outline of
a plan that he would soon unveil. In short, he had the best possible platform from which to launch a viable and effective assault
on global hunger.

Beginning his twelve-hour workdays in Rome and a globe-
hopping schedule, McGovern immediately received a respectful
hearing from heads of state, foreign ministers, and other ambas-
sadors. Since his diplomatic duties were linked to the humanitarian efforts of agencies of the United Nations and not the political agenda of any one nation, he was free to take a truly global,
politically less-encumbered view of his responsibilities and opportunities. As ambassador, he was "always dealing globally—from
morning until night, . . . with global problems other than the problems of [just] Italy or India or Japan or Saudi Arabia," he recalled
in 2003. "[I was] constantly thinking in worldwide terms." Calling
his experience as ambassador "deeply rewarding, deeply satisfy-

George and Eleanor McGovern hold hands on the campus of Dakota Wesleyan University in May 1997.

ing," he noted that the "global framework obviously expanded my range of interests and activities."[14]

Guided by this expanded vision, McGovern began a tour of the world's most impoverished regions, where hunger was chronic and of epidemic proportions. In trips to Africa, Asia, the Middle East, Western Europe, and elsewhere, McGovern was afforded the opportunity to assess firsthand the wide range of political, cultural, and environmental contexts in which hunger persisted. He also encountered many positive actions that were being taken to address these problems. These were "mind-expanding and soul-expanding experiences" for him.[15] Two trips, in particular, captured McGovern's imagination, fueling his desire to develop a practical strategy to expand the battle against world hunger.

In 1999, he traveled to Siberia, which he had always imagined as a frozen wilderness. He found, rather, a vast agricultural land not unlike much of his native South Dakota. In this vast heartland, however, lived people who were surprisingly poor. Such misery in the midst of plenty jolted both his consciousness and conscience, bringing back memories of poverty he had witnessed in America earlier in his life on the American Indian reservations of the Great Plains and in the rural areas of the Deep South.[16]

The next year, he made his first trip to mainland China, where he encountered two distinct "Chinas." The first was the east coast, home to ancient cities that still reflect some of the grandeur of centuries-old civilizations but are now transforming into high-tech, industrial centers of the new global economy. Along this "gold coast," especially in its major cities, the world's most populous nation is vying for a significant role as a major producer and consumer of goods and services. Just fifty miles into the interior, however, another country exists. This China, where the majority of the nation's population lives, is as poor as almost anywhere else on earth. Here, McGovern saw children without adequate food, housing, and medical care. Visiting one schoolroom in western China, he noticed that half the children were standing as the teacher took them through their lessons:

> I finally said to the teacher, "Why don't the children sit down?"
> He said, "We don't have enough desks for that." They actually

had no desks, as we would see it. They were seated on little cross beams—two children on each beam—and then a slate in their laps to write on. But there were only enough seats for half the children, so each hour they would trade places. During that five- or six-hour school day, they were standing half the time. There was no school lunch. There [were] not even any toilet facilities, which is one of the reasons, I was told, why little girls tend to drop out of school when they get to be eight or nine or ten years of age. Boys tend to run out behind the schoolhouse and look for a tree or bush or something. But that's difficult for little girls, and so they stay at home in some cases. Now that's poverty in a country that is thriving on the east coast—one of the great trading countries in the world now. That experience showed me . . . the vast amount of work we still have to do, [and] not only in China.[17]

McGovern's trips to these former and future superpowers continued to disturb his conscience, focus his mind, and stoke his passion to end the curses of hunger and poverty. Among the key issues that increasingly dominated his thinking was the plight of women and girls in the world's poorest regions, where they play the primary roles in producing and distributing food. McGovern realized that educated women are much less vulnerable to the problems of poverty and, therefore, more likely to escape the web of hunger. This understanding led him to a fascinating link between the education of girls and food. In many of the cultures where hunger is chronic, biases exist that lead to the valuing of education for boys, but not girls. However, when food is available at school, parents are often willing to set aside their cultural bias and send their daughters to school rather than see them starve.[18] The fight against hunger amongst school-aged children is also, therefore, a fight for the future well-being of women in these cultures. Understanding this dimension of the puzzle has provided additional political and cultural leverage for McGovern's cause.

In addition to his trips to Russia and China, McGovern's experiences in central Africa also weighed heavily on his mind:

I saw in Africa something that both frightened and disturbed me, and that was the AIDS epidemic. It's kind of like a great locomotive roaring across the countryside without brakes and no warning lights and no traffic control—just slaying people right and left. I walked through villages in Africa where there are no people, let us say, between the ages of 20 and 60 that are left. The mothers and fathers are gone, and what you have are large numbers of orphans, plus the grandparents trying as best they can to rear the children. [This] terrible epidemic [is] worse than the bubonic plague and other plagues of history.[19]

While McGovern viewed the AIDS epidemic in Africa as a human catastrophe in its own right, he also saw it as another piece to the puzzle of hunger. Because much of the epidemic is centered in agricultural areas, he discovered, it kills both farmers (the food producers) and homemakers (the primary food distributors), exacerbating the problem of hunger in rural areas.

Back home, the events of 11 September 2001 suggested another piece to the puzzle of hunger and poverty. The ambassador had been in Paris having lunch with the editors of the *International Herald Tribune* when he learned of the attacks in New York City and Washington, D.C. Why, he asked his lunch mates, and for months later himself, would the attackers of the World Trade Center and the Pentagon "despise us as much as they do? The president says it's because they hate our freedom and that they're cowards who were willing to try to destroy it." McGovern, however, did not "think they were cowards. I think they were misguided, terribly misguided. I don't justify what they did, but the question is 'why?' Why is there this anger that drives terrorist attacks against a country we believe is the greatest country in the world?" The answer, he realized, lay in the contrast between the misery of much of the world's population and the life we live as Americans:

They see the misery of their people, the deaths of little children from hunger and disease, and then they see the opulence and the luxury [of] some [in] their own governments, and they see the incredible luxury and sometimes outright waste involved in the lifestyles of the West, especially in America. They see it in our movies, they see it on the village television screen, they read about it, and they're infuriated that their people . . . live such miserable lives. . . . In order to unleash that anger they sign on to a religious fanatic like Osama bin Laden and strike back at the symbols of western financial and military power. But I think, if we're ever . . . to get at the root causes of terrorism, we have to look at the misery and anger that drives it.[20]

As he put the pieces of the global puzzle of hunger and poverty together, the South Dakotan also began to mobilize the power that came from his official role as a United States ambassador, a power that was multiplied by his status as an elder statesman. McGovern felt relatively unencumbered by the bureaucracy that normally limits the authority of diplomats. His "chain of command" was his conscience and his global vision. "I really stood, for the four years I was in Rome, for what I thought was in the best interest of the people of the planet," he recalled. One way in which he bypassed the usual bureaucratic barriers was to make public statements that put the United States government at center stage and in a position of having to make a commitment one way or the other. For instance, McGovern proposed publicly that the United States take the lead within the United Nations framework in providing a good, nutritious daily lunch for every hungry schoolchild in the world. "I didn't clear that at the State Department level," he said. "I didn't clear it at the White House. I just started talking about it and writing articles about it, buttonholing people, and enlisting [former political allies like] Bob Dole."[21]

It was this global school-lunch initiative that finally coalesced into a comprehensive, economically feasible, and politically practical plan to eradicate hunger. McGovern outlined his plan in 2001 with publication of *The Third Freedom: Ending Hunger in Our Time.* The title of the book refers to Franklin D. Roosevelt's State of the Union Address in 1941, in which the president spoke of four essential freedoms that required defending against the threat of global fascism. They included (1) freedom of speech and expression, (2) freedom to worship, and (4) freedom from fear of aggression. The third of Roosevelt's essential freedoms was freedom from "want." In McGovern's view, it was time for America, in partnership with the global community, to liberate the hungry of the world from the scourge that robbed them of this essential freedom.

After making his case for the seriousness of the problem and why he believed it was not so vast and endemic as to be beyond practical solution, McGovern outlined a nine-point plan. In addition to calling for agricultural assistance to developing countries, he challenged the United States to work with the United Nations in instituting universal school-lunch programs and nutritional programs for pregnant mothers and their preschool children.[22]

Some planks of the plan were clearly logical extensions of work already envisioned, or even begun, by the United States government, the United Nations, or international aid agencies. Other aspects of the proposal, and the sheer audacity of the goal to end global hunger in a generation, sprang from McGovern's intellect and passion.

While ambitious, the plan—especially the global school-lunch program and the project to support women, infants, and children—almost immediately garnered support from across the political spectrum and throughout the world. In the United States, the formidable pair of George McGovern and Robert Dole, whose bipartisan partnership had successfully fought hunger in America decades earlier, began to loosen the government's purse strings. Together, McGovern stated in 2003, he and Dole got nearly "half a billion dollars out of the federal government to undertake feeding hungry children in 38 different countries. . . . And that would never have happened had I not just seized the day and went ahead with the idea.[23] Ambassador McGovern's audacity in challenging the United States government to take up his call to arms against global hunger had begun to pay off. Even after the George W. Bush Administration relieved McGovern of his diplomatic post in 2001, Congress continued to support the McGovern-Dole global school-lunch program, lending government sanction to McGovern's proposals and impetus for other governments and aid agencies to join the cause.

When McGovern left his post as ambassador to the United Nations Food and Agriculture Organization in Rome, the United Nations World Food Programme (WFP) took the unprecedented step of naming him global ambassador on hunger. Both the offer and McGovern's acceptance of this role marked a mutual commitment to the plan McGovern had described in *The Third Free-*

dom. Catherine Bertini, WFP executive director (and later under-secretary general for operations at the UN), announced McGovern's appointment. "As a WFP founder and long-time supporter, he is ideally placed to help ensure that hunger remains at the top of the humanitarian agenda," she stated. "I can't think of anyone better than George McGovern to serve as our first ambassador. At a time like this, when it is more important than ever we find long-term ways to solve world hunger, I am proud he will be at our side."[24] By the summer of 2003, McGovern had already attended a number of international conferences in his new role, including a conference in Geneva, Switzerland, on rural development. He also attended a conference in Rome called to assess the United Nations' progress toward meeting the goal set at the 1996 World Food Summit, which had called for halving the number of chronically hungry persons in the world by 2015.[25]

A Prophetic and Unencumbered Voice

While a high-school student in Mitchell, South Dakota, George McGovern joined the debate team to help him overcome his natural shyness. It must have worked, because McGovern has rarely been reticent in expressing his opinions since that time. Throughout his political life, McGovern's rhetoric exhibited the edginess of a true populist representing causes and persons that he held dear. Always a tough-minded, honest, and forthright thinker, he now carries the weight of prophet and elder. He speaks unashamedly and boldly as someone whose wisdom has been honed and needs to be reckoned with by friend and foe alike.[26] He also speaks for those who have no political voice—namely the poor and dispossessed, especially the children. Increasingly, and with growing fervor, he speaks for those who do not yet even have a voice—future generations.

Although he appears from time to time on television talk shows (such as Larry King's) and plans to write at least one more book, the press is McGovern's medium of choice, particularly major metropolitan newspapers and leading magazines. Within the past few years, however, he has also discovered the power of electronic media to multiply the effects of almost anything written in the traditional press. In late 2002, for example, McGovern's "The Case for Liberalism: A Defense of the Future against the Past" appeared in *Harper's Magazine*. Because he served on its board of directors, McGovern knew the magazine had a modest circulation. Even so, he kept meeting people who had read the article. When he asked if they were subscribers, they inevitably replied that they had picked the article up on the Internet or received a copy by e-mail. He came to realize that "you can reach several million people with one article in a way that wouldn't have been possible ten years ago, or even five years ago." While admitting that he was not completely comfortable with "all these new fangled gadgets," McGovern acknowledged that the new technology enabled "those articles I've written and some of the op-ed pieces I've written for the *L A Times* and the *Wall Street Journal* and *New York Times* and *Washington Post*" to gain wider circulation. "I find those [articles] laying on people's desks or I see them being discussed on television. I know that's one way that I can be effective," he concluded in 2003.[27] This phenomenon, the e-version of the grassroots politics that McGovern's political life has long exemplified, signifies how his voice continues to resonate with the ideas and ideals of each new generation of Americans and in each new medium.[28]

Two pieces McGovern wrote in 2002 and 2003, in particular, have found responsive audiences. The first was "The Case for Liberalism," in which he argued that the philosophy of conservatism, by its very nature, cannot and historically has not changed American culture into a "more just and equitable society." Rather, it is the philosophy of liberalism, McGovern claims, that can provide a "practical and hopeful compass by which to guide the American ship of state."[29] The second piece, "The Reason Why," was published by *The Nation*. The title of the article was taken from two lines of Alfred Lord Tennyson's famous poem "The Charge of the Light Brigade:" "Theirs not to reason why,/Theirs but to do and die."[30] In this criticism of the Bush Administration's decision to wage war in Iraq, McGovern argues that there does indeed *need* to be a voice that demands to know the reason why.

Together, these articles provide a platform from which McGovern can play the elder statesman's role. His purpose is not merely to represent the other side of the issue. Nor is he acting only as a social commentator or political pundit. Rather, he means to provide historical, philosophical, and even moral perspectives on the crucial social and political issues of the day. At this stage in his life and work, he strives to pass on wisdom, insight, and hope to the future even as he speaks forcefully to the perceived mistakes of the present.

To Keep the Dreams Alive

Only history can record the ultimate legacy of George McGovern, for the United Nations global ambassador on hunger still plans to be on the job as long as he can manage. At ceremonies marking the founding of the George and Eleanor McGovern Library and Center for Public Service at Dakota Wesleyan University, McGovern was asked how he, at age seventy-nine, was able to accomplish his remarkable activities as the United States ambassador to the United Nations Food and Agriculture Organization in Rome. Pausing for a moment to reflect, he replied, "My work on hunger these past few years has probably been the thing that has kept me alive."[31]

When asked about that statement in September 2003, McGovern recalled the words of actress Katherine Hepburn, who had passed away that summer at age ninety-six. "She said something like this," McGovern answered, "and I think this is verbatim: 'You have to keep going—I've been as terrified as the next person, but you have to keep the dreams alive." As a much younger and angrier man, Senator McGovern had once exclaimed, "I'm sick and tired of old men dreaming up wars in which young men do the dying."[32] As an elder statesman, he continues to question the reasons for going to war. He dreams of ending global hunger, and his work keeps thousands upon thousands of children from dying. To be true to his legacy is to keep his dream alive.

NOTES

1. Telephone interview with George McGovern, Mitchell, S. Dak., 11 Sept. 2003.

2. Another prime example would be President Jimmy Carter.

3. *See* Max Weber, *The Theory of Social and Economic Organization*, trans. A. M. Henderson and Talcott Parsons (New York: Oxford University Press, 1947), pp. 64–65.

4. Interview with McGovern, 11 Sept. 2003.

5. American Business Council of the Gulf Countries, *The Gulf Report Online 3* (Spring 1999), abcgc.org/newsleter/spring99/, accessed 17 June 2004.

6. Robert Sam Anson, *McGovern: A Biography* (New York: Holt, Rinehart, & Winston, 1972), p. 4.

7. I once asked Eleanor and George whether they thought his war record would it have made a difference if used in the campaign. They just looked at each other for a moment and then changed the subject.

8. "A Journey into the Wild Blue Yonder with WWII Pilot George McGovern," *BookPage*, Aug. 2001, www.bookpage.com/0108bp/stephen_ambrose.html, accessed 17 June 2004.

9. Richard M. Marano tells the story of McGovern and the 1984 Democratic campaign in *Vote Your Conscience: The Last Campaign of George McGovern* (Westport, Conn.: Praeger, 2003).

10. U. S. Mission to the U.N./Rome, www.usembassy.it/usunrome/files/mcgovern.htm, accessed 18 June 2004.

11. "Middle East Policy Council: About," www.mepc.org/public_asp/about.asp, accessed 6 July 2004.

12. U. S. Mission to the U.N./Rome. As the director of Food for Peace, McGovern convinced Kennedy to support the fledgling WFP. McGovern's appointment as ambassador gave him the chance to work once more with the United Nations, an institution he admired. In 1976, he had been appointed by President Gerald R. Ford as delegate to the thirty-first session of the UN General Assembly. In 1978, President Jimmy Carter appointed him as a delegate for the Special Session on Disarmament.

13. In August 2000, McGovern received the Presidential Medal of Freedom from President Bill Clinton, who called McGovern "one of the greatest humanitarians of our time" (quoted in "The Medal of Freedom," 9 Aug. 2000, cbsnews.com/stories/2000/08/09/national/printable223205.shtml, accessed 18 June 2004). In October of the same year, the World Food Programme presented him with the first "Food for Life" Award in recognition of "his outstanding contribution to ending global hunger" ("George McGovern: New Award for America's Humanitarian Hero," www.usembassy.it/usunrome/files/Statements/award.htm, accessed 17 June 2004).

14. Interview with McGovern, 11 Sept. 2003.

15. Ibid.

16. Ibid.

17. Ibid.

18. George McGovern, *The Third Freedom: Ending Hunger in Our Time* (New York: Simon & Schuster, 2001), pp. 30–31.

19. Interview with McGovern, 11 Sept. 2003.

20. Ibid.

21. Ibid.

22. McGovern, *Third Freedom*, pp. 159–61.

23. Interview with McGovern, 11 Sept. 2003.

24. "George McGovern to be WFP's First Ambassador," 26 Oct. 2001, www.europaworld.org/issue54/georgemcgovern261001.htm, accessed 17 June 2004.

25. "World Food Summit, 13–17 November 1996, Rome, Italy," www.fao.org/wfs/main_en.htm, accessed 6 July 2004; "World Food Summit: Five Years Later Reaffirms Pledge to Reduce Hunger," www .fao.org/worldfoodsummit/english/newsroom/news/8580-en.html, accessed 6 July 2004.

26. "Over the years," he noted recently, "I have developed some skill in telling the difference between, as Lyndon Johnson put it, 'chicken salad and chicken shit'" (McGovern, "The Case for Liberalism: A Defense of the Future against the Past," *Harper's Magazine* 305 [Dec. 2002]: 37).

27. Interview with McGovern, 11 Sept. 2003.

28. McGovern reported that one woman told him she enclosed copies of his *Harper's* article in her Christmas cards to five hundred people. Interview with McGovern, 11 Sept. 2003.

29. McGovern, "The Case for Liberalism," p. 39.

30. Quoted in McGovern, "The Reason Why," *The Nation*, 21 Apr. 2003, p. 20.

31. McGovern, "The Third Freedom: Ending Hunger in Our Time" (speech, L. B. Williams Elementary School, Mitchell, S.Dak., 4 May 2001).

32. Interview with McGovern, 11 Sept. 2003.

CHAPTER NINE

COME HOME, AMERICA

THE LEGACY OF GEORGE McGOVERN

THOMAS J. KNOCK

 On an evening during the twilight summer of his administration, President William Clinton presided for the last time over an annual White House event that he had always found gratifying. Into the East Room, he and First Lady Hillary Rodham Clinton welcomed some two hundred guests to recall the achievements of fourteen special Americans who were about to receive the nation's highest civilian honor, the Medal of Freedom. The fourteen included Daniel Patrick Moynihan, retiring senator from New York and presidential adviser since the Kennedy era; Mathilde Krim, pioneering AIDS activist and researcher; Jesse Jackson, the dynamic civil-rights leader; John Kenneth Galbraith, one of the twentieth century's most influential economists; Marian Wright Edelman, the indefatigable champion of underprivileged children; General Wesley Clark, lately commander of United Nations forces in the Kosovo conflict; and George McGovern.

"Day in and day out," Mrs. Clinton said, the individuals being celebrated "have widened our horizons and opened our minds and our hearts." Both he and his wife, the president added, had played a role in the selections: "Some of them reflect, now that we've been . . . involved in public life for nearly three decades, a lot of personal experiences that we have had, and we had a lot of good times talking about who should be here today."[1] Clinton was no doubt thinking of his experiences with the former Democratic standard bearer in whose presidential campaign he and the First Lady had worked twenty-eight years earlier, but memories of 1972 were not the real reason that the then ambassador to the United Nations Food and Agriculture Organization was among those being honored that night in August 2000. "War hero, Senator, diplomat, George McGovern embodies national service," the Medal of Freedom citation read. It also acknowledged the Distinguished Flying Cross that his brave exploits had earned him during World War II, his "stalwart voice for peace in Vietnam," and his unwavering "commitment to bring food to the hungry." The commendation thus concluded: "George McGovern is one of the greatest humanitarians of our time, and the world will benefit from his legacy for generations to come."

In all respects, the words were fitting and unexaggerated. And yet, naturally, no formal tribute, no matter how felicitous, could adequately convey the fullness or assess the legacy of a career of the historical significance of George McGovern's. Nor, it must be admitted, could a single essay. But in striving toward that goal, one might begin by quoting perhaps the most telling phrases in the Medal of Freedom citation—"the power of his example, the courage of his convictions."[2]

An Important Voice from the Beginning

There is no more striking illustration of those phrases than, appropriately, McGovern's first speech on the floor of the Senate, on 15 March 1963, delivered barely four months after the Soviet-American confrontation had teetered at the brink of thermonuclear war. Entitled "Our Castro Fixation versus the Alliance for Progress," the address began by defending President John F. Kennedy against right-wing attacks for his disinclination to undertake a post-missile-crisis invasion of Cuba. At the same time, however, McGovern did not fear to characterize as a "tragic mistake" the administration's own trespasses against that island (in particular, the Bay of Pigs invasion). He then offered an inventory of Latin America's real problems—that the richest two percent of the people controlled half the region's wealth, while 80 percent lived in shacks or huts; that the rate of illiteracy exceeded one-third; and that disease and malnourishment plagued 50 percent of its people. He also cited the burdens of swelling populations, one-crop economies, unjust tax structures, and military establishments designed to keep the system intact. History might honor Fidel Castro, the senator proffered, because his revolution had at least "forced every government of the hemisphere to take a new and more searching look at the crying needs of the great masses of human beings." As for his fellow citizens, they should not dissipate their energies "in a senseless fixation on Castro." Instead, their mission ought to be "to point the way to a better life for the hemisphere and . . . for all mankind." Nor should they forget that there were promises to keep at home as well as around the globe. The nation's unfinished domestic agenda involved the work of creating new jobs and greater educational opportunities for young people; of securing civil-rights legislation; of doing something about rising medical and hospital costs confronting older people; and of stimulating a sluggish economy. "It is no longer possible," the senator said, "to separate America's domestic health from our position in world affairs."[3]

Anticipating his condemnation of the Vietnam War and his reputation as a left-leaning liberal, McGovern's debut in the Senate would seem to have launched him upon a trajectory from which he would rarely stray. In time, the country's entanglement in Southeast Asia would further sharpen his convictions about the potentialities and shortcomings of liberal reform in America. Coming at the high tide of Vital Center liberalism,[4] his observations about the impact of foreign policy on the quality of life in the United States were unusual, even bold, and they seem no less instructive some forty years later. Yet, his coupling of peace and progressive change was not just premonitory; the idea that foreign policy and domestic policy were virtually symbiotically linked— a conception from which his chief political legacy inheres—also had roots in his own past.[5]

Early Influences

The son of a conservative Wesleyan Methodist minister, George McGovern grew up in Mitchell, South Dakota, during the Great Depression. Whereas his upbringing in a religious household was undoubtedly the central influence on his personal development, the nation's economic calamity ran a close second. One of his earliest memories, at the age of ten, was of seeing a grown man cry. The incident occurred when George and his father paid a call on their friend, Art Kendall, a hard-working local farmer. As they drove up, Kendall sat sobbing on the back porch steps. In his hand, he held the check he had just received for his entire year's production of hogs. Like a story out of the Populist era, the amount of the check did not even cover the cost of shipping the hogs to market, let alone the feed to get them ready. McGovern would encounter other circumstances of hardship and heartache during these hard times, but this one, which "choked a farmer's spirit and sent him into bankruptcy," would stay with him forever.[6]

As for his early formal education, it was perhaps not surprising that, when he studied American history at Mitchell High School, he could not help being impressed with the statesmen of his own part of the country. He especially admired men such as Peter Norbeck, Robert La Follette, and George Norris, who strove to lessen the burdens of farmers, laborers, and small businessmen. A gifted history teacher, Bob Pearson, encouraged the teenager's interest in the past and persuaded him to join the debate team. At length, Pearson became the main factor behind McGovern's decision to major in history at Dakota Wesleyan University, where he enrolled in the fall of 1940 and evolved into a star debater of considerable regional renown. Not incidentally, debate became his means of social ascent as well as his introduction to politics. In honing his forensic skills from 1938 to 1943, he necessarily immersed himself in the study of controversial events and subjects that defined the era—in propositions that ranged from whether the country's railroad system should be nationalized to whether the United States and Great Britain should form a permanent alliance.[7]

Eventually, of course, the war would interrupt his string of debate victories, along with a rather idyllic campus life. In February 1943, the United States Army Air Forces called him to train as a B-24 bomber pilot. Over Germany, Italy, and Austria, he flew thirty-five combat missions. For his steady courage and skill—most conspicuously for an emergency landing on a tiny island in the Adriatic and for another harrowing predicament that required him to bring in his disabled plane on one tire—he was awarded the Distinguished Flying Cross. He would also carry away indelible memories of human suffering wrought of war (especially of Italian children on the edge of starvation) that were far more extreme than anything he had ever beheld in South Dakota.[8]

McGovern had shipped overseas inspired "by the vision of Roosevelt and Churchill and . . . the United Nations," he once recalled. Returning home in 1945, he felt as if he was about "to participate in the launching of a new day in world affairs."[9] His wartime experiences had heightened his desire to study American history and international relations. With the help of the GI Bill, he entered the Ph.D. program at Northwestern University. His professors included Ray Allen Billington, the distinguished intellectual historian; Richard Leopold, one of the early deans of diplomatic history; and L. S. Stavrianos, a specialist in Eastern European history who would acquaint him with the decisive role that the Soviet Union had played in defeating Nazi Germany. Then there was the young Arthur S. Link, the great Woodrow Wilson biographer. Link would become McGovern's dissertation supervisor and lifelong friend, and the professor's devotion to the subjects of Progressive reform and American internationalism influenced his graduate student in both subtle and conclusive ways. But McGovern also admired the works of the Progressive historians of the previous generation — practitioners such as Vernon L. Parrington and Charles A. Beard — who emphasized, not consensus (as Link did), but the role that conflict had played in bringing about change in American history. In this regard, McGovern's dissertation topic, "The Colorado Coal Strike of 1913–14," is instructive. The story of the ruthless war that John D. Rockefeller, Jr., conducted against the Colorado miners and their families resonated for McGovern, reminding him of those in South Dakota who had struggled against economic and political forces beyond their control. Through the process of reconstructing the great coalfield war, his view of politics and social conflict was beginning to crystallize, forming the intellectual context in which he would embrace the cause of civil rights and the antiwar movement.[10]

Crucially, McGovern's academic studies engendered a preference for critical analysis and ideas. If one sought a better world, then one had to cultivate a *serious* sense of history in order to arrive at a useful understanding of American politics. And the same principle surely held in the realm of American foreign policy. Thereon, his reading included Owen Lattimore, E. H. Carr, Edwin Reischauer, and John K. Fairbank, whose scholarly works raised doubts in his mind about the nature of the burgeoning Cold War. Like many of his peers and professors, McGovern supported Henry Wallace for president in 1948, though he became somewhat disillusioned with the former secretary of agriculture because of the fanatical elements that had commandeered his campaign.[11] Even so, before long, McGovern had reached the conclusion that the Cold War was the result, as he said in a letter to Arthur Link, "of U. S. blundering and allegiance to reactionary regimes on the one hand and Soviet stubbornness and opportunism on the other hand." Indeed, he wrote his mentor in September 1950, in light of the Truman Administration's support for General Franco, Chiang Kai-shek, and Syngman Rhee, America's course appeared to have been flawed since the death of Franklin Roosevelt. "We seem to be unaware that two thirds of the world is either in revolution or on the verge of it" (a fact which the Soviets easily grasped and exploited), whereas "we are engaged in a hopeless process of sitting on the lid in the tension centers of the world." What with the Korean Conflict and McCarthyism, he feared as well for "what ever liberalism remains in the United States."[12]

History's Loss, the Democrats' Gain

By 1953, McGovern had earned his Ph.D. and accepted a position at Dakota Wesleyan University. But politics had become such an irresistible attraction that his teaching career proved as short-lived as it was highly successful. "What a loss to history!" Arthur Link exclaimed when he heard the news that McGovern had resigned a tenure-track job to take up the task of reorganizing the then-moribund Democratic party of South Dakota.[13] And moribund the party was. Only the year before, the staunchly conservative state had given Dwight D. Eisenhower a two-to-one margin of victory over Adlai Stevenson and elected 108 Republicans to the 110-seat state assembly. Its governor and its two congressmen and United States senators were Republicans, as well. Nevertheless, by 1956, McGovern had not only revived competitive two-party politics, but he also managed to win election to the United States House of Representatives.[14]

The freshman did not waste time making his presence known. No sooner had he ascended Capitol Hill than he offered an important amendment to a farm bill that would have established 90-percent parity payments; though the amendment failed of adoption by a mere four votes, the folks back home were duly impressed. The following year, a different McGovern proposal did become law. In its original form, the National Defense Education Act of 1958 would have provided federal loans to college students concentrating in the sciences. The former history professor, however, argued that the nation would be better served by extending those benefits to all students regardless of major. The Committee on Education and Labor was persuaded; the amended legislation was enacted; and part of the foundation for full-scale federal aid to education in the next decade had been laid.[15]

Because of initiatives of this sort, as well as attentive constituency work and an appealing personal manner, McGovern won re-election in 1958. He was also assisted by Ezra Taft Benson, the maladroit secretary of agriculture who had undermined the Democrats' regime of price supports. Practically every day, McGovern said, he "took a bite out of" Benson.[16] Apparently, he had also voiced the concerns of South Dakotans effectively enough so that they were willing to forgive his outspoken opposition to key aspects of the administration's foreign policy. For example, he voted against the Eisenhower Doctrine, a pledge to protect American interests in the Middle East through military aid or intervention. Such a course, McGovern believed, left untouched the social and political problems ("the swamplands of poverty and disease") that threatened the region's peace. How, he wondered, could America use its resources to sustain despots "who embody everything that is alien to our tradition of liberty and equality" and "who seek to freeze the status quo"? The real test of foreign aid, he declared, ought to be "how effectively it enables the people of the underdeveloped areas to build up the kind of society where better standards of life are possible."[17] Both the Eisenhower Doctrine and McGovern's stand against it, each in its own way, were harbingers of things to come.

By 1960, McGovern was ready to challenge Karl Mundt, the conservative, two-term Republican incumbent, for his seat in the

Senate. In November, John F. Kennedy would lose South Dakota to Richard Nixon by fifty thousand votes (out of over three hundred thousand), whereas McGovern would come within fifteen thousand of capsizing Mundt.[18] Defeat contained within it a rare opportunity. The following January, President Kennedy appointed McGovern the director of Food for Peace. This program had been established in 1954 primarily to alleviate the burden of America's grain surpluses by distributing them abroad. Eisenhower's critics called it a dumping program. In contrast, Kennedy's charge to his special assistant was to make "the most vigorous and constructive use possible" of America's agricultural abundance in order to narrow the gap between the haves and the have-nots.[19]

The assignment was perfect for McGovern. Under his direction, Food for Peace would undergo a vast expansion and public-relations makeover, molded both by earnest humanitarian impulses and New Frontier anti-Communism. For nearly two years, he traveled constantly, overseeing allotments of hundreds of thousands of tons of food and fiber that would be used as "self-help capital" to fuel labor-intensive economic development projects. In twenty-one Third World countries, Food for Peace provided partial wage payments for seven hundred thousand workers engaged in land clearance, reforestation, irrigation, and reclamation and in the construction of bridges, dams, roads, schools, and hospitals.[20] For McGovern, this was the way to fight the Cold War. "American food," he liked to say, "has done more to prevent . . . communism than all the military hardware we have shipped around the world."[21]

Dearest to his heart, however, was the overseas school-lunch program, which he worked extremely hard to revitalize. Among other things, the director's dedication resulted in dramatic improvements in school attendance and in the health of legions of malnourished children. By 1962–1963, the children at the Food for Peace table numbered one million in Peru, two million in Korea, three-and-a-half million in Egypt, four-and-a-half million in Brazil, nine million in India, and over ten million in Southeast Asia. McGovern had thus supervised arguably the greatest humanitarian achievement of the Kennedy and Johnson administrations. In the program's combination of idealism and pragmatism, McGovern had demonstrated by vivid example his own vision of what the United States ought to be doing in the Third World, the new stage upon which the Cold War was being played out. The experience (which shaped his inaugural Senate speech) would have a lasting impact on his thinking about the ways powerful nations figure in the lives of weaker ones.

Making Full Use of a Senator's Pulpit

Despite his success, McGovern still longed to be a senator. With President Kennedy's blessings, he entered the race in South Dakota in 1962 and won. The initial stage of his new apprenticeship occurred during the promising interlude between the Cuban Missile Crisis and the expansion of the war in Vietnam. The prevailing state of international relations, McGovern believed, held the possibility both of curbing the nuclear arms race and of dismantling (at least partially) America's colossal military-industrial complex through a gradual shift in the nation's economy toward more pacific industrial enterprises.

In the summer and fall of 1963, the senator introduced extraordinary legislation to serve these ends. In two speeches, he proposed for fiscal 1964 a $5 billion cut in defense appropriations, which then stood at $53.6 billion, or well over half the entire federal budget. He made a powerful case for pruning. In every category of nuclear weaponry, the United States far outpaced Soviet capabilities. He cited Secretary Robert McNamara's recent admission that an all-out nuclear exchange would yield fatalities "on the order of 300 million," emphasizing that the two superpowers together had amassed the equivalent of from forty to sixty billion tons of TNT in their nuclear stockpiles—enough to kill every living thing on the face of the earth many times over. In light of such excessive "'overkill' capacity," McGovern asked, "what possible advantage" could accrue from "appropriating additional billions of dollars to build more missiles and bombs"?[22] The time had come for a fundamental reconsideration of national security needs and their implications for American society. What, in this instance, could a $5 billion savings mean? "[I]t would build a $1 million school in every one of the nation's 3,000 counties," he answered, "plus 500 hospitals costing $1 million apiece, plus college scholarships worth $5,000 each to 100,000 students—and still permit a tax reduction of a billion dollars."[23]

Not far from McGovern's mind was President Eisenhower's theretofore uncelebrated Farewell Address, in which the retiring president had warned against "the conjunction of an immense military establishment and a large arms industry," which "is new in the American experience."[24] The influence of this warning was manifest in another McGovern initiative entitled the National Economic Conversion Act, introduced in October 1963. Counseling a coordinated effort between industry and government, the bill called for a presidential commission to identify "any reasonable future opportunities for converting the instruments of war to the tools of peace." Systematic planning was the key in the coming transition: it would at once relieve the anxieties of all concerned who had grown dependent upon the Pentagon; it would "add new force to disarmament discussions by removing fear of the economic consequences"; and it could "cause a boom, rather than a drag on our economy." Leavening his remarks with allusions to Eisenhower, he presented evidence that the current level of military spending distorted the economy, weakened the competitive position of civilian industries, and aggravated the balance of payments problem.[25] As he had pointed out in an earlier speech, the United States had slipped from first to fifth place in machine-tool production. Meanwhile, Japan and western Europe were busy modernizing their civilian industrial plant at a far faster rate than American manufacturers. Then, too, thousands of public school teachers were failing to meet reasonable teaching standards. Apart from everything else, then, a reordering of priorities seemed a matter of common sense.[26]

Chiefly because of Vietnam, McGovern's perception of a "peace dividend" was fleeting. Yet, he would always contend that the Cold War could not be won by military means. Ironically, in September 1963, in the speech in which he explained how much a diversion of just 10 percent ($5 billion) of the defense budget could accomplish at home, he referred to "the current dilemma in Vietnam" as "a clear demonstration of the limitations of military power." The current budget of over $50 billion was apparently no match for "a ragged band of illiterate guerrillas fighting with homemade

weapons" against the tyrannical government in Saigon, which existed only because the United States had created and financed it.
President Kennedy's policy was scarcely one of victory or even
stalemate, he observed; rather, it was "a policy of moral debacle
and political defeat." He ended this, the earliest trenchant commentary on the subject by any senator, with a prophetic warning:
"[T]he failure in Vietnam will not remain confined to Vietnam.
The trap we have fallen into there will haunt us in every corner
of this revolutionary world if we do not properly appraise its lessons. . . . [and] rely less on armaments and more on the economic,
political, and moral sources of our strength."[27]

McGovern's previous assignment also had a bearing on his
alarm. Only five weeks before, he had received disturbing information from the American embassy in Saigon. Food for Peace had
become integral to the feeding of militia trainees in the Strategic
Hamlet program and other counterinsurgency efforts, the charge
d'affaires reported. In order "to maintain a high level of military
expenditures for the prosecution of the war," moreover, the pro-
ceeds from the sale of the food were being delivered over to Ngo
Dinh Diem.[28] Actually, while it would suffer across-the-board cuts
elsewhere, McGovern's cherished project was being dramatically
stepped up in South Vietnam. Under Lyndon Johnson, as much as
half of the total program would be diverted to subsidize the Saigon
government; under Richard Nixon, the proportion would swell to
two-thirds. Food for Peace, the senator grieved, had become "Food
for War."[29]

Vietnam Critic

In August 1964, as the presidential contest between Lyndon
Johnson and Barry Goldwater was commencing, McGovern voted
in favor of the Gulf of Tonkin Resolution, mainly for the sake
of the Great Society but nonetheless with great misgivings. Even
before Johnson's inauguration, McGovern would begin to air his
concerns on the floor of the Senate. In January 1965, in an extended historical review of American involvement, he implored
the administration to pursue negotiations with Hanoi and then
laid out a five-point program for bringing Ho Chi Minh to the conference table under the auspices of the United Nations.[30] The pro-

posal made headlines throughout the country. Two months later, CBS News invited McGovern to take part in a prime-time televised debate. In response to his hawkish copanelists, he denounced the prospect of escalation and massive bombing as worse than futile, predicting "a staggering loss of life out of all proportion to the stakes involved. . . . [and] such enormous instability . . . that indeed we invite a much worse situation than the one that exists." It would be far better, he also said, "for politicians to take some political risks than for us to risk a course that might cost the lives of hundreds of thousands of our citizens."[31]

The senator well understood that the strongest piston in the engine that drove the war was domestic politics—that is, the baleful repercussions of McCarthyism in tandem with Johnson's fear of a right-wing backlash at home that would undermine his loftier ambitions. In most respects, it was Kennedy's and Nixon's fear, too; from Truman onward, no president was willing to permit the Communist dominos to fall under his watch, or otherwise preside over an American military defeat, in Southeast Asia.[32] Initially, McGovern was not unsympathetic, and he tried to reason with President Johnson in private. On one such occasion in the Oval Office, he endeavored to refute the Johnsonian article of faith that Ho Chi Minh was a surrogate of Red China. Drawing on his own careful study, McGovern stressed the fact that the Vietnamese and the Chinese had hated each other for a thousand years and that Ho might well serve as a dependable barrier against Chinese expansion. "Goddamn it, George," Johnson interrupted after about three minutes, "I don't have time to be sitting around this desk reading history books."[33]

In other circumstances, McGovern almost certainly could have been counted among the president's staunchest supporters, for their domestic aspirations for the American people were barely distinguishable. Yet there was a fundamental difference. Johnson believed that in order to conduct his war on poverty he must also fight Communism in Southeast Asia, whereas McGovern believed that in order to achieve a truly great society the United States must refrain from, or at least curtail, military interventionism in the name of anti-Communism. Events would bear out the senator. Over the next two years, the administration continued to prop up a quasi-dictatorship in Saigon, while B-52s rained down upon Vietnam over a million tons of bombs, a magnitude exceeding the tonnage dropped by all the belligerents in World War II. Nearly sixteen thousand American soldiers lost their lives in the blood-soaked jungles as troop levels climbed to five hundred thousand, and perhaps that many Vietnamese were killed. And, at home, domestic turmoil engulfed the United States on a scale not seen since the Civil War.[34]

By this juncture, McGovern had emerged as one of the leading critics of the war within the liberal establishment. In April 1967, for example, in "The Lessons of Vietnam," one of the most penetrating speeches of his career, he pronounced the conflict "the most tragic diplomatic and moral failure in our national experience," for it was "degenerating into a defeat for America whether we 'win' or 'lose'." Only "by a crude misreading of history and a distortion of our most treasured ideals" could anyone defend this war, he said, which was "essentially a civil conflict among various groups of Vietnamese." In any case, the challenge of Communism could not be met "by forcing an American solution on a people still in search of their own national identity." And if it did not end soon, the consequences both at home and abroad would be severe. "Our dreams of a Great Society and a peaceful world will turn to ashes." Congress, he concluded, "must never again surrender its power under our constitutional system by permitting an ill-advised, undeclared war," thus rendering its function "very largely one of acquiescence."[35]

In 1968, despite the Democrats' disastrous convention in Chicago (where he had launched a last-minute campaign for the presidential nomination at the behest of Robert Kennedy's bereft disciples), McGovern was reelected to the Senate by a comfortable margin. In the first half of his second term, he realized two major achievements. As chair of his party's commission to review the rules on delegate selection, he was instrumental in opening up that process so that significant numbers of women, blacks, and younger people for the first time could participate meaningfully. The reform commission's recommendations were controversial, to say the least, and their ultimate impact was probably as great on the Republicans as on the Democrats.[36] Then, in keeping with his own sense of priorities, he pushed through the Congress a dramatic expansion of the then underfunded domestic school-lunch and food-stamp programs. His legislation doubled the former and quadrupled the latter and led to the establishment of nutrition standards, including the federal requirements that we have today for the listing of nutrition facts on the labels of all packaged foods. Among his chief allies in these projects was Senator Robert Dole.[37]

The war, however, remained McGovern's most abiding concern. Even though President Nixon had begun a piecemeal reduction of troop levels, the bombing, destruction, and human slaughter approached (and would soon surpass) the enormity of the Johnson years.[38] His patience all but exhausted, McGovern wondered just how long the search for "peace with honor" was going to take. In the spring of 1970, he began to look for a legislative solution. On 30 April—just hours before Nixon ordered the surprise United States invasion of Cambodia—McGovern and his Republican cosponsor, Mark Hatfield of Oregon, introduced a measure to cut off funds for the war within six months and to withdraw all American combat troops from Southeast Asia by the end of 1971. This first serious attempt by either house of Congress to reclaim its constitutional prerogatives with regard to the power to declare war and to raise and support armies was the culmination of years of frustration among many members. More specifically, it proceeded from McGovern's perspective that the war, while killing Americans and Vietnamese by the tens of thousands, was also devouring precious resources and degrading the quality of American life and politics. Unemployment and inflation had almost doubled since Johnson left office. Nixon had vetoed health and education bills, dragged his feet on food stamps, and, as part of his southern electoral strategy, had attempted to place on the Supreme Court two enemies of civil rights. McGovern and Hatfield were troubled, as well, by the sense of alienation and powerlessness that had begun to permeate the antiwar movement.

In the wake of the shootings at Kent State on 4 May, the McGovern-Hatfield Amendment won the cosponsorship of twenty-five senators and became the pivot of a wide variety of groups arrayed against the war. During the summer-long debate, thousands of young people came to Washington to lobby on its behalf, while the White House pulled out all the stops in trying to thwart the measure and discredit its authors. Just before the final roll call on 1 September, McGovern told his colleagues and the audience in the gallery above that the "cruelest, the most barbaric" war in American history was no less the property of the Congress than it was of Nixon. "This chamber reeks of blood," he declared, in a rare public display of emotion. "Every Senator here is partly responsible for the human wreckage at Walter Reed and Bethesda Naval and all across our land—young boys without legs, or arms, or genitals, or faces, or hopes. . . . And if we don't end this foolish, damnable war, those young men will some day curse us for our pitiful willingness to let the Executive carry the burden that the Constitution places on us."[39]

By a vote of fifty-five to thirty-nine, the amendment failed— because, according to Hatfield, "senators saw it as too radical." Nonetheless, the size of the protest, at 42 percent, was significant. Nixon, unlike his predecessors, would now have to cope with the fact that he was losing public support. In this respect, as Hatfield interpreted, the results marked "the beginning of the end of the Vietnam War."[40] The measure laid the basic groundwork for the War Powers Act, as well.

The outcome disappointed McGovern, but he was also gratified by the fact that, in trying to do what he believed needed to be done, millions of people had stood behind the endeavor. And so the seed was planted—the only way to change the policy was to change the White House. In January 1971, he announced his candidacy for president and began to wage what one might call a campaign for progressivism and peace. Those twin goals, it is worth emphasizing, demarcated the logical common ground uniting the political coalition that responded so fervently to his grassroots campaign and helped him capture the Democratic nomination on the first ballot. For most of the elements that made up that constituency, as for McGovern himself, foreign policy and domestic reform were coefficients. Peace in Southeast Asia was essential to change at home, and vice versa.

Over the next year and a half, the candidate would present to his fellow citizens what amounted to an extended, critical treatise on what has been called the American Century. In his acceptance speech in Miami, he promised to end the war within ninety days, pare down the defense budget, and curtail military adventurism. He also pledged to expand opportunities for higher education, advance the cause of women's rights, create a fairer tax structure and health care system, and ensure that every able-bodied citizen had a job provided by either the private sector or the federal government. In this way, the United States might "become again a witness to the world for what is noble and just in human affairs." Both as a people and as a member of the world community, the nation's historic potentiality was indivisible. "So join with me in this campaign," he bade the ebullient delegates. "Lend me your strength and your support — and together, we will call America home to the ideals that nourished us in the beginning."[41]

Retirement?

Although the ill-fated campaign met with resounding defeat, South Dakota returned George McGovern to the Senate in 1974, three months after Nixon resigned from office in disgrace. A year later, in part because of the residual impact of McGovern's campaign and Watergate, Congress at last pulled the props out from under America's longest war. The senator continued in the late 1970s to speak out against the arms race and foreign interventions and pressed his case that population control and feeding the world's hungry ought to be priorities second only to the prevention of nuclear war. In his bid for a fourth term, he became the main target of the National Conservative Political Action Committee and, along with several other liberal Senate Democrats, was overwhelmed in the Reagan landslide in 1980. In "retirement," in addition to serving as president of the Middle East Policy Council, he lectured on college campuses, spoke on radio and television, and wrote two books and a host of magazine articles. In a sense, neither the issues nor his views on them had changed substantively. In foreign policy, for instance, in the 1990s he was advocating a form of Wilsonian internationalism rather than a post-Cold War incarnation of unilateralist globalism.

Then, in 1997, President Clinton appointed him ambassador to three United Nations agencies dealing with international food and agricultural issues. At his post in Rome, McGovern set about

McGovern distributes food among school children in India during a tour of the area in January 1976, testifying to his lifelong commitment to ending hunger in the world. Photograph by R. N. Khanna

formulating a plan to lift half the world's underfed population out of the grip of hunger by 2015. The mission was under way by May 2000, when he persuaded President Clinton to pledge significant resources to start an international school-lunch program for the world's 300 million malnourished children. A few weeks before the Medal of Freedom ceremonies, McGovern presented the proposal to the Senate Agriculture Committee with Bob Dole at his side. He also wrote a book, *The Third Freedom*, in which he lamented the fact that, at the turn of the new millennium, an astonishing 31 million Americans did not have enough to eat. He explained how it was possible to end hunger in the world, entirely, if only the United States, in cooperation with the United Nations, decided that it wanted to do so.[42] In the fall of 2001, he accepted an invitation from the United Nations to become its "Global Ambassador on Hunger."

Soon thereafter, having maintained a period of respectful silence, he began to criticize the George W. Bush Administration. For example, in the pages of *Harper's Magazine*, he issued a remarkable summons to Democrats in "The Case for Liberalism." He opened the essay by extolling the great legislative achievements engendered by that philosophy during the presidencies of Theodore Roosevelt, Woodrow Wilson, Franklin Roosevelt, and Lyndon Johnson, implying that today's leading liberal politicians might have something to learn from these men. He then turned to the Bush Administration, which was, he said, "devoted to killing progressive programs while spending lavishly on the military and cutting taxes for the rich." He went on to reprove the administration for rejecting the Kyoto accords to halt global warming, for abrogating the ABM Treaty of 1972 ("the cornerstone of worldwide arms control"), and for abandoning true cooperation with the United Nations and the World Court for "a go-it-alone policy that is obsolete in today's interdependent world." As for the incipient war with Iraq, he questioned the administration's claims about that country's weapons of mass destruction and its alleged connections to Osama bin Laden, reminding his readers that, nevertheless, "international law does not give the President of the United States, or any other head of state, the right of 'preventive' war." Regarding terrorism and rising enmity for America, he asked, "Is the fact that half the people of the world live in poverty perhaps the key to terrorism? Is it possible that we cannot reduce terrorism except as we reduce poverty in the world?"

In his closing paragraphs, Ambassador McGovern recalled some of the horrific scenes he had witnessed during his combat service in World War II and wished that more members of the Bush Administration had had some kind of battlefield experience so that they might come to appreciate the words of Edmund Burke: "A conscientious man would be cautious how he dealt in blood." And, characteristically, McGovern argued that, with careful planning, the military budget could be cut by one third and thus provide a leaner, more efficient defense. The billions of dollars saved could be spent to create a national health-care policy and improve the public school system, to develop renewable sources of energy, and to repair the nation's brittle infrastructure and build a modern system of rail transportation. "I firmly believe that if we were to take such steps," he concluded, "America would be a better defended, more secure, happier nation than it is today."[43]

A Life's Work

In all of it aspects, this most recent chapter in Ambassador McGovern's career is distinguished by a kind of symmetry. Yet, even if he had not been afforded the opportunity to return to Rome and the World Food Programme and to advance the cause of "freedom from want," there still would remain the fact that he accomplished more on behalf of people in need than have most presidents and secretaries of state in American history. His life remains an ongoing testament to his creed "that one person, despite weaknesses and mistakes, can make a difference," as he put it in his autobiography,[44] as well as to "the power of his example," as underscored by the Medal of Freedom text.

The presidential citation aptly paid homage to "the courage of his convictions," upon which McGovern's legacy also rests. In a recent CNN interview about Iraq, McGovern poignantly remarked to Judy Woodruff, "I don't enjoy criticizing the policies of my government. I love this country more than life itself."[45] With undiminished resolve, he carries on in his reliance upon first principles and in his understanding of the past in defense of the future, just as he did from his first days as a congressman to his final months in the Senate. For what impelled McGovern to speak out and often stand alone then are basically the same things that motivate him now in his early eighties. One cannot help wondering whether he has found some satisfaction in the prophetic elements of so many of the positions he has taken through the decades. Indeed, most concluding chapters of studies of the Vietnam War read as if they were paraphrasing the corpus of his speeches on that subject. Then, too, who could question "the courage of his convictions" when he enjoined his fellow citizens and those who exercised power in their name to try to gain historical perspective on the issues or to consider other means besides force in the making of American foreign policy? The propositions that he asked Americans to consider in the 1960s and 1970s continue to hold implications for interventionism in the Third World, for the armaments race and the use of force in international relations, for the political economy of the United States relative to other industrial powers, and, not least, for the nature of the nation's political and social institutions.

Perhaps for some, McGovern's legacy is as yet unclaimed. But it is there, nonetheless, in its intrinsic and tangible qualities alike—a life's work driven by an unrelenting sense of duty to explore alternative approaches to the ideas and institutions that forged the American Century and an enduring faith in the possibilities for national redemption through authentic internationalism, education, and humanitarian endeavor. In 2004 and beyond, George McGovern continues to beckon, "Come Home, America."

NOTES

1. Both quoted in Jacqueline L. Salmon, "The President's Honor Roll," *Washington Post*, 10 Aug. 2000, p. C4.

2. "The President Presents the Nation's Highest Civilian Honor, the Medal of Freedom, to Senator George McGovern," copy of citation, author's collection.

3. McGovern, "Our Castro Fixation vs. the Alliance for Progress," 88th Cong., 1st sess., *Congressional Record* 109 (15 Mar. 1963): 96–102. A version of the speech under McGovern's byline appears as "Is Castro an Obsession with Us?," *New York Times Sunday Magazine*, 19 May 1963, pp. 9, 106–9.

4. *See* Arthur M. Schlesinger, Jr., *The Vital Center: The Politics of Freedom* (Boston: Houghton Mifflin Co., 1949).

5. Much of the material presented in this essay is based on research in, among other sources, the George McGovern Papers, located in the Seeley Mudd Library, Princeton University, Princeton, N.J.; and on a series of personal interviews with McGovern and others. For a more detailed provisional overview, *see* Thomas J. Knock, "Come Home, America: The Story of George McGovern," in *Vietnam and the American Political Tradition: The Politics of Dissent*, ed. Randall B. Woods (Cambridge, U.K.: Cambridge University Press, 2003), pp. 82–120.

6. McGovern, *The Third Freedom: Ending Hunger in Our Time* (New York: Simon & Schuster, 2001), pp. 20–21.

7. McGovern, *Grassroots: The Autobiography of George McGovern*, pp. 12–13, and Knock, "Come Home, America: The Story of George McGovern," pp. 86–87.

8. *See* Steven E. Ambrose, *The Wild Blue: The Men and Boys Who Flew the B-24s over Germany* (New York: Simon & Schuster, 2001), p. 128.

9. Interview with McGovern, 9 Aug. 1991.

10. Ibid.; Knock, "Come Home, America: The Story of George McGovern," pp. 88–90.

11. McGovern, *Grassroots*, pp. 40–42.

12. McGovern to Link, 19 Aug., 30 Sept. 1950, Arthur S. Link Papers, Seeley Mudd Library, Princeton University, Princeton, N.J.

13. Link, quoted in author's interview with William H. Harbaugh, 23 Oct. 1995.

14. Robert Sam Anson, *McGovern: A Biography* (New York: Holt, Rinehart & Winston, 1972), pp. 63–90; Alan L. Clem, *Prairie State Politics: Popular Democracy in South Dakota* (Washington, D.C.: Public Affairs Press, 1967), pp. 38–40. "More than any other figure," Clem observes, McGovern was "responsible for the existence of both a partisan and ideological choice in contemporary South Dakota politics" (p. 55).

15. McGovern, *Grassroots*, pp. 77–78.

16. Interview with McGovern, 1 Oct. 1991. *See also* Jon K. Lauck, "George S. McGovern and the Farmer: South Dakota Politics, 1953–1962," *South Dakota History 32* (Winter 2002): 331–53.

17. McGovern speeches, quoted in Knock, "Come Home, America: The Story of George McGovern," pp. 93–94.

18. Anson, *McGovern*, pp. 91–98.

19. Quoted in McGovern, *Third Freedom*, p. 51.

20. This discussion of Food for Peace is based on the author's "Feeding the World and Thwarting the Communists: George McGovern and

Food for Peace," in *Architects of the American Century: Individuals and Institutions in 20th Century U. S. Foreign Policymaking,* ed. David F. Schmitz and T. Christopher Jespersen (Chicago: Imprint Publications, 2000), pp. 98–120.

21. Quoted ibid, p.109.

22. "New Perspectives on American Security," 2 Aug. 1963, reprinted in McGovern, *A Time of War, A Time of Peace* (New York: Vintage Books, 1968), pp. 5–22, quotations on pp. 6, 11.

23. McGovern, "A Proposal to Reverse the Arms Race," 24 Sept. 1963, reprinted ibid., pp. 24–35, quotation on p. 28.

24. Eisenhower, "Farewell Address," 17 Jan. 1961, reprinted at www .netlibrary.com, accessed 1 July 2004.

25. McGovern, "The National Economic Conversion Act," 31 Oct. 1963, reprinted ibid., pp. 49–60, quotations on pp. 49, 54, 57.

26. McGovern, "Proposal to Reverse the Arms Race," pp. 32–33.

27. Ibid., pp. 29, 34.

28. William C. Trueheart, quoted in Knock, "Feeding the World," p. 110.

29. Ibid., pp. 112–13. It is interesting to note that recent scholarly works focusing on South Vietnam at the local level have made a strong case that the United States lost the war even before the escalation—chiefly because policy makers ignored the concerns of those who lived the agrarian life, especially landless peasants. Conversely, the National Liberation Front made irreversible inroads in the countryside in part by either slashing exorbitant rents or seizing the large holdings of absentee landlords and distributing them among the tenants. *See* Eric M. Bergerud, *The Dynamics of Defeat: The Vietnam War in Hau Nghia Province* (Boulder, Colo.: Westview Press, 1991), pp. 2, 12–23, 54–68, 82–84, and David W. P. Elliott, *The Vietnamese War: Revolution and Social Change in the Mekong Delta, 1930–1975,* 2 vols. (Armonk, N.Y.: M. E. Sharpe, 2003), 1:440–43.

30. Knock, "Come Home, America: The Story of George McGovern," pp. 104–5.

31. Transcript, CBS News Special Report, "Vietnam: The Hawks and the Doves," 8 Mar. 1965, Speeches and Statements 1965, McGovern Papers.

32. Virtually every scholarly assessment of American involvement in the war makes this argument.

33. Quoted in interview with McGovern, 29 Dec. 1992. One could argue that reading about Vietnam is exactly what Johnson needed to be doing. As none other than Daniel Ellsberg observed in 1972, "There has

never been an official of Deputy Assistant Secretary rank or higher (including myself) who could have passed in office a midterm freshman exam in modern Vietnamese history" (Ellsberg, *Papers on the War* [New York: Simon & Schuster, 1972], p. 28n.16). Three years later, James C. Thomson, Jr., a member of the National Security Council from 1961 to 1967, wrote, "[T]he American government was sorely *lacking in real Vietnamese or Indochina expertise*" (Thompson, "How Could Vietnam Happen?," in *Who We Are: An Atlantic Chronicle of the United States and Vietnam*, ed. Robert Manning and Michael Janeway [Boston: Little, Brown & Co., 1969], p. 200). In 1994, Republican senator Mark Hatfield of Oregon, contemptuous of the presumption of both Kennedy and Johnson and their advisers that "raw military power" might prevail, remarked, "Those people were thinking in terms of World War II. . . . They had little knowledge [of Vietnam] and never read Mao on guerrilla warfare or anybody else" (interview with Mark Hatfield, 7 Oct. 1994).

34. The literature on this topic is enormous, but good books to start with include: George C. Herring, *America's Longest War: The United States and Vietnam, 1950–1975*, 3d ed. (New York: McGraw-Hill, 1996); Fredrik Logevall, *Choosing War: The Lost Chance for Peace and the Escalation of War in Vietnam* (Berkeley: University of California Press, 1999); and David Kaiser, *American Tragedy: Kennedy, Johnson, and the Origins of the Vietnam War* (Cambridge, Mass.: Belknap Press, 2000).

35. "The Lessons of Vietnam," 25 Apr. 1967, reprinted in McGovern, *Time of War, A Time of Peace*, pp. 128–145; quotations on pp. 129–31, 143–45.

36. *See* Stephen K. Ward, "George McGovern and the Promise of a New Democrat: Reform and National Politics in the Democratic Party, 1968–1970," in this volume.

37. McGovern, *Grassroots*, pp. 168–69; Anson, *McGovern*, pp. 218–42; interviews with McGovern, 7 Aug. 1993, and Dole, 27 Nov. 2001.

38. The two most authoritative studies are Jeffrey Kimball, *Nixon's Vietnam War* (Lawrence: University Press of Kansas, 1998), and Larry Berman, *No Peace, No Honor: Nixon, Kissinger, and Betrayal in Vietnam* (New York: Free Press, 2001).

39. Quoted in Knock "Come Home, America: The Story of George McGovern," p. 116.

40. Quoted ibid., pp. 116–17. This discussion of the amendment is also based on the author's "The Beginning of the End: George McGovern and the Amendment to End the War," a paper presented at the 86th Annual Meeting of the Pacific Coast Branch of the American Historical Association, Aug. 1995.

41. McGovern, "Come Home, America" (acceptance speech), 13 July 1972, reprinted in *An American Journey: The Presidential Campaign Speeches of George McGovern* (New York: Random House, 1974), p. 23. For the campaign, *see* Jon D. Schaff, "A Clear Choice: George McGovern and the 1972 Presidential Race," in this volume. Gary Warren Hart's *Right from the Start: A Chronicle of the McGovern Campaign* (New York: Quadrangle, 1973) remains the best book-length study; but *see also* Theodore H. White, *The Making of the President, 1972* (New York: Atheneum Publishers, 1973).

42. McGovern, Preface to *Third Freedom*, pp. 11–14.

43. McGovern, "The Case for Liberalism: A Defense of the Future against the Past," *Harper's Magazine* 305 (Dec. 2002): 37–42.

44. McGovern, *Grassroots*, p. 197.

45. "McGovern: 'What's the Big Hurry?'" (interview transcript), 13 Feb. 2003, www.cnn.com/2003/ALLPOLITICS/02/13/cnna.mcgovern.ip/index.html, accessed 2 July 2004.

A CHRONOLOGY OF THE LIFE OF
GEORGE STANLEY MCGOVERN

LAURIE LANGLAND

19 JULY 1922
   Born to Rev. Joseph McGovern and Frances McLean
      McGovern at Avon, South Dakota
1928
   Family moves to Mitchell, South Dakota, after living in
      Calgary, Alberta, Canada
1940
   Graduates from Mitchell High School
   Enrolls at Dakota Wesleyan University, Mitchell
1943–1945
   Serves in United States Army Air Forces as a B-24 pilot
31 OCTOBER 1943
   Marries Eleanor Stegeberg of Woonsocket, South Dakota
1945
   Receives Distinguished Flying Cross
   Daughter Ann born
1946
   Daughter Susan born
   Graduates with honors from Dakota Wesleyan University
   Attends Garrett Theological Seminary in Evanston, Illinois
   Serves as student minister at Diamond Lake, Illinois
1949
   Daughter Teresa ("Terry") born
1950
   Accepts teaching position at Dakota Wesleyan University
1952
   Son Steven born
1953
   Earns Ph.D. in history and government from Northwestern
      University

On Main Street of Mitchell, South Dakota, McGovern's children and their friends rally support for his reelection to Congress in 1958.

Becomes executive secretary of the South Dakota Democratic
Party

1955

Daughter Mary born

1956

Elected to United States House of Representatives, defeating
Harold Lovre

1958

Reelected to House, defeating Joe Foss

1960

Loses election for United States Senate to Karl Mundt

Appointed as director of Food for Peace Program by
President John F. Kennedy

1962

Elected to Senate, defeating Joe Bottum

1963

Becomes first person to challenge the Vietnam War on Senate
floor

1965

Tours Vietnam, which solidifies his commitment to ending
war

1967

Awarded honorary Doctor of Laws degree by Dakota
Wesleyan University

1968

Announces candidacy for the presidency

Loses nomination to Hubert Humphrey

Reelected to the Senate, defeating Archie Gubbrud

1969

Accepts chairmanship of Commission on Party Structure and
Delegate Selection

1970

Cosponsors McGovern-Hatfield legislation to end Vietnam
War

Sponsors Food Stamp Reform Act as part of effort to end
hunger in America

1971

Formally declares candidacy for president

McGovern campaigns outside his childhood home in Avon, South Dakota.

1972
   Wins Democratic presidential nomination
   Loses election to Richard Nixon
1974
   Reelected to third Senate term, defeating Leo Thorsness
1976
   Named delegate to United Nations General Assembly by
      President Gerald Ford
1978
   Appointed as Senate delegate to United Nations Special
      Session on Disarmament by President Jimmy Carter
1980
   Loses Senate election to James Abdnor
1980–1985
   Founds and chairs Americans for Common Sense, a
      public-interest group
1981–1995
   Serves as visiting professor at Columbia University,
      Northwestern University, Cornell University, American
      University, and University of Berlin, among others
1984
   Runs for Democratic presidential nomination but withdraws
      from race
1991–1998
   Serves as president of Middle East Policy Council
1994
   Daughter Terry dies
1998
   Appointed ambassador to United Nations Food and
      Agriculture Organization by President Bill Clinton
2000
   Awarded Presidential Medal of Freedom by President Clinton
2001
   Appointed first global ambassador on hunger by the United
      Nations World Food Programme

SELECTED BIBLIOGRAPHY

Abramowitz, Alan I. "Explaining Senate Election Outcomes."
    American Political Science Review 82 (June 1988): 385–403.
Abramson, Paul R., John H. Aldrich, and David W. Rohde.
    "Progressive Ambition among United States Senators: 1972–1988."
    Journal of Politics 49 (1987): 3–35.
Alexandratos, Nikos, ed. *World Agriculture: Towards 2010: An FAO
    Study.* Chichester, England: Food and Agriculture Organization of
    the United Nations, John Wiley & Sons, 1995.
Alsop, Stewart. "A Conversation with Nixon aboard Air Force One."
    Newsweek, 4 Sept. 1972, pp. 24–26.
Ambrose, Stephen E. *The Wild Blue: The Men and Boys Who Flew the
    B-24s over Germany.* New York: Simon & Schuster, 2001.
Anson, Robert Sam. *McGovern: A Biography.* New York: Holt,
    Rinehart & Winston, 1972.
Austin, James E. *Nutrition Programs in the Third World: Cases and
    Readings.* Cambridge, Mass.: Oelgeschlager, Gunn & Hain, 1981.
Bearak, Barry. "Why People Still Starve." *New York Times Magazine,*
    13 July 2003, pp. 32–37, 52, 60–61.
Beck, Kent M. "What Was Liberalism in the 1950s?" *Political Science
    Quarterly* 102 (Summer 1987): 233–58.
Bergerud, Eric M. *The Dynamics of Defeat: The Vietnam War in Hau
    Nghia Province.* Boulder, Colo.: Westview Press, 1991.
Berman, Larry. *No Peace, No Honor: Nixon, Kissinger, and Betrayal in
    Vietnam.* New York: Free Press, 2001.
Bishop, Jim. *FDR's Last Year: April 1944–April 1945.* New York:
    William Morrow & Co., 1974.
Boller, Paul F., Jr. *Presidential Anecdotes.* New York: Oxford University
    Press, 1981.
Boyne, Walter J. *Beyond the Wild Blue: A History of the United States Air
    Force, 1947–1997.* New York: St. Martin's Press, 1997.
Cathie, John. *The Political Economy of Food Aid.* New York: St. Martin's
    Press, 1982.

Cavala, William, and Austin Ranney. "Changing the Rules Changes the Game." *American Political Science Review* 68 (Mar. 1974): 27–42.

Clem, Alan L. *Government by the People?: South Dakota Politics in the Last Third of the Twentieth Century.* Rapid City, S.Dak.: Chiesman Foundation for Democracy, 2002.

———. *Prairie State Politics: Popular Democracy in South Dakota.* Washington, D.C.: Public Affairs Press, 1967.

———. *South Dakota Political Almanac,* 2d ed. Vermillion, S.Dak.: Dakota Press, 1969.

———. "Variations in Voting Blocs across Policy Fields: Pair Agreement Scores in the 1967 U.S. Senate." *Western Political Quarterly* 23 (1970): 530–51.

Cohn, Theodore H. *Global Political Economy: Theory and Practice.* 2d ed. New York: Longman, 2003.

Democratic National Committee. Papers. Presidential Libraries, National Archives, Washington, D.C.

Democratic Party. Democratic Peace Caucus File, Sept.–Dec. 1967. Library of Congress, Washington, D.C.

Diamond, Robert A., ed. *Congressional Quarterly Almanac: 92nd Congress, 1st Session, 1971.* Washington, D.C.: Congressional Quarterly, 1972.

Dutton, Frederick G. *Changing Sources of Power: American Politics in the 1970s.* New York: McGraw-Hill Book Co., 1971.

Edsall, Thomas Byrne. *The New Politics of Inequality.* New York: W. W. Norton & Co., 1984.

Elliott, David W. P. *The Vietnamese War: Revolution and Social Change in the Mekong Delta, 1930–1975.* 2 vols. Armonk, N.Y.: M. E. Sharpe, 2003.

Elliott, Larry. "The Lost Decade," *Guardian,* 9 July 2003.

Ellsberg, Daniel. *Papers on the War.* New York: Simon & Schuster, 1972.

Fenno, Richard, Jr. *Home Style: House Members in Their Districts.* Boston: Little, Brown & Co., 1978.

Foote, Joseph, ed. *The Presidential Nominating Conventions, 1968,* Washington, D.C.: Congressional Quarterly Service, 1968.

Hart, Gary Warren. *Right from the Start: A Chronicle of the McGovern Campaign.* New York: Quadrangle, 1973.

Hauffe, Rick. "McGovern is Natural Leader." *South Dakota Hall of Fame* 20 (Fall 1994): 28.

Heckscher, August. *Woodrow Wilson: A Biography*. New York: Charles Scribner's Sons, 1991.

Herring, George C. *America's Longest War: The United States and Vietnam, 1950–1975*. 3d ed. New York: McGraw-Hill, 1996.

Hitzhusen, Fred J. "Context, Concepts and Policy on Poverty and Inequality." In *Food, Security and Environmental Quality in the Developing World*, ed. Rattan Lall et al., pp. 419–28. Boca Raton, Fla.: Lewis Publishers, 2003.

Kaiser, David. *American Tragedy: Kennedy, Johnson, and the Origins of the Vietnam War*. Cambridge, Mass.: Belknap Press, 2000.

Karolevitz, Robert F. "Life on the Home Front: South Dakota in World War II." *South Dakota History* 19 (Fall 1989): 392–423.

Kimball, Jeffrey. *Nixon's Vietnam War*. Lawrence: University Press of Kansas, 1998.

Kirkpatrick, Jeane. *The New Presidential Elite: Men and Women in American Politics*. New York: Russell Sage Foundation & Twentieth Century Fund, 1976.

Knock, Thomas J. "Come Home, America: The Story of George McGovern." In *Vietnam and the American Political Tradition: The Politics of Dissent*, ed. Randall B. Woods, pp. 82–120. Cambridge, U.K.: Cambridge University Press, 2003.

———. "Feeding the World and Thwarting the Communists: George McGovern and Food for Peace." In *Architects of the American Century: Individuals and Institutions in Twentieth-Century U.S. Foreign Policy-making*, ed. David F. Schmitz and T. Christopher Jespersen, pp. 98–120. Chicago: Imprint Publications, 2000.

Kutzner, Patricia L. *World Hunger: A Reference Handbook*. Santa Barbara, Calif.: ABC-CLIO, 1991.

Lauck, Jon K. "George S. McGovern and the Farmer: South Dakota Politics, 1953–1962." *South Dakota History* 32 (Winter 2002): 331–53.

Lee, Loyd E. *World War II*. Greenwood Press Guides to Historic Events of the Twentieth Century. Westport, Conn.: Greenwood Press, 1999.

Leech, Margaret. *In the Days of McKinley*. New York: Harper & Bros., 1959.

Lengle, James I., and Byron Shafer. "Primary Rules, Political Power, and Social Change." *American Political Science Review* 70 (Mar. 1976): 25–40.

Lichtman, Allan J., and Ken DeCell. *The Thirteen Keys to the Presidency.* New York.: Madison Books, 1990.

Lillibridge, G. D. ("Don"). "Small-Town Boys: Growing Up in Mitchell in the 1920s and 1930s." *South Dakota History* 25 (Spring 1995): 1–36.

Lindell, Terrence J. "Populists in Power: The Problems of the Andrew E. Lee Administration in South Dakota." *South Dakota History* 22 (Winter 1992): 345–65.

Link, Arthur S. Papers. Seeley Mudd Library, Princeton University, Princeton, N.J.

Logevall, Fredrik. *Choosing War: The Lost Chance for Peace and the Escalation of War in Vietnam.* Berkeley: University of California Press, 1999.

McClelland, Donald G. *U. S. Food Aid and Sustainable Development: Forty Years of Experience.* USAID Program and Operations Assessment Report No. 22. N.p: U.S. Agency for International Development, 1998.

McGovern, Eleanor, with Mary Finch Hoyt. *Uphill: A Personal Story.* Boston: Houghton Mifflin Co., 1974.

McGovern, George S. *An American Journey: The Presidential Campaign Speeches of George McGovern.* New York: Random House, 1974.

———. "The Case for Liberalism: A Defense of the Future against the Past." *Harper's Magazine* 305 (Dec. 2002): 37–42.

———. Foreword to *Give Peace a Chance.* Ed. Melvin Small and William D. Hoover. Syracuse, N.Y.: Syracuse University Press, 1992.

———. Foreword to *The L Word,* by David P. Barash. New York: William Morrow & Co., 1992.

———. Foreword to *Power & Light: Political Strategies for the Solar Transition,* by David Talbot and Richard E. Morgan. New York: Pilgrim Press, 1981.

———. *Grassroots: The Autobiography of George McGovern.* New York: Random House, 1977.

———. "Is Castro an Obsession with Us?" *New York Times Sunday Magazine,* 19 May 1963, pp. 9, 106–9.

————. "The Lessons of 1968." *Harper's Magazine* 240 (Jan. 1970): 43–47.

————. Papers. Seeley Mudd Library, Princeton University, Princeton, N.J.

————. "The Reason Why." *The Nation*, 21 Apr. 2003, pp. 18, 20–21.

————. *Terry: My Daughter's Life-and-Death Struggle with Alcoholism.* New York: Random House, Villard Books, 1996.

————. *The Third Freedom: Ending Hunger in Our Time.* New York: Simon & Schuster, 2001.

————. *A Time of War, A Time of Peace.* New York: Random House, Vintage Books, 1968.

————. *War against Want: America's Food for Peace Program.* New York: Walker & Co., 1964.

McGovern, George S., and Leonard F. Guttridge. *The Great Coalfield War.* Boston: Houghton Mifflin, 1972.

McGovern, George S., ed. *Agricultural Thought in the Twentieth Century.* Indianapolis, Ind.: Bobbs-Merrill Co., Inc., 1967.

————, ed. *Food and Population: The World in Crisis.* Great Contemporary Issues series. New York: Arno Press for the *New York Times*, 1975.

MacLaine, Shirley. *McGovern: The Man and His Beliefs.* New York: W. W. Norton & Co., 1972.

McNamara, Robert S., with Brian VanDeMark. *In Retrospect: The Tragedy and Lessons of Vietnam.* New York: Times Books, 1995.

Marano, Richard M. *Vote Your Conscience: The Last Campaign of George McGovern.* Westport, Conn.: Praeger, 2003.

Matthews, Donald R. "The Folkways of the United States Senate: Conformity to Group Norms and Legislative Effectiveness." *American Political Science Review* 53 (1959): 1064–89.

Maxwell, Simon. "The Disincentive Effect of Food Aid: A Pragmatic Approach." In *Food Aid Reconsidered: Assessing the Impact on Third World Countries*, ed. Edward Clary and Olav Stokke, pp. 66–90. London: Frank Cass, 1991.

Miller, Warren E., and Donald E. Stokes. "Constituency Influence in Congress." *American Political Science Review* 57 (1963): 45–56.

Moore, John L., ed. *Congressional Quarterly's Guide to U.S. Elections*, 2d ed. Washington, D.C.: Congressional Quarterly, 1990.

Morris, Edmund. *The Rise of Theodore Roosevelt*. New York: Coward, McCann & Geoghegan, 1979.

Nevins, Allan, ed. *The Burden and the Glory: The Hopes and Purposes of President Kennedy's Second and Third Years in Office as Revealed in His Public Statements and Addresses*. New York: Harper & Row, 1964.

New York Times, 1943–1972.

Newsweek, 10 July 1972–6 Nov. 1972.

Nichols, Roy Franklin. *Franklin Pierce: Young Hickory of the Granite Hills*. Philadelphia: University of Pennsylvania Press, 1931.

Ornstein, Norman J., Thomas E. Mann, and Michael J. Malbin, eds. *Vital Statistics on Congress, 1989–1990*. Washington, D.C.: Congressional Quarterly, 1990.

Peabody, Robert L., Norman J. Ornstein, and David W. Rohde. "The United States Senate as a Presidential Incubator: Many Are Called but Few Are Chosen." *Political Science Quarterly* 91 (Summer 1976): 237–58.

Peirce, Neal R. *The Great Plains States of America: People, Politics, and Power in the Nine Great Plains States*. New York: W. W. Norton & Co., 1972.

Phillips, Kevin P. *The Emerging Republican Majority*. New Rochelle, N.Y.: Arlington House, 1969.

Phreno Cosmian, 18 Dec. 1940–24 Mar. 1942.

Pierce, Franklin. Papers. Manuscripts Division, Library of Congress, Washington, D.C. Presidential Papers Microfilm, 1959.

Pierre Daily Capital Journal, 17 July 1972.

Podhoretz, Norman. *Breaking Ranks: A Political Memoir*. New York: Harper & Row, 1979.

Polsby, Nelson W. *Consequences of Party Reform*. New York: Oxford University Press, 1983.

Poole, Keith T., and Steven R. Daniels. "Ideology, Party, and Voting in the U.S. Congress, 1959–1980." *American Political Science Review* 79 (1985): 373–99.

Radosh, Ronald. *Divided They Fell: The Demise of the Democratic Party, 1964–1996*. New York: Free Press, 1996.

Rauh, Joseph. Papers. Library of Congress, Washington, D.C.

Rohde, David W. "Risk-Bearing and Progressive Ambition: The Case

of Members of the United States House of Representatives."
American Journal of Political Science 23 (Feb. 1979): 1–26.

Ruttan, Vernon W. "The Politics of U. S. Food Policy: A Historical Review." In *Why Food Aid?*, ed. Ruttan, pp. 1–36. Baltimore: Johns Hopkins University Press, 1993.

Salmon, Jacqueline L. "The President's Honor Role," *Washington Post*, 10 Aug. 2000.

Scammon, Richard M., and Ben J. Wattenberg. *The Real Majority*. New York: Coward-McCann, 1970.

Schlesinger, Arthur M., Jr. *The Vital Center: The Politics of Freedom*. Boston: Houghton Mifflin Co., 1949.

Schlesinger, Stephen C. *The New Reformers: Forces for Change in American Politics*. Boston: Houghton Mifflin Co., 1975.

Shafer, Byron E. *Quiet Revolution: The Struggle for the Democratic Party and the Shaping of Post-Reform Politics*. New York: Russell Sage Foundation, 1983.

Shaw, D. John. *The UN World Food Programme and the Development of Food Aid*. Houndsmill, England: Palgrave, 2001.

————, and Edward Clay, eds. *World Food Aid: Experiences of Recipients & Donors*. Rome: World Food Programme, 1993.

Singer, Hans, John Wood, and Tony Jennings. *Food Aid: The Challenge and the Opportunity*. Oxford: Clarendon Press, 1987.

Small, Melvin. *The Presidency of Richard Nixon*. Lawrence: University Press of Kansas, 1999.

Stanley, Robert G. *Food for Peace: Hope and Reality of U. S. Food Aid*. New York: Gordon & Breach, 1973.

State of Food Insecurity. Rome: Food and Agriculture Organization, 2002.

Thompson, James C., Jr. "How Could Vietnam Happen?" In *Who We Are: An Atlantic Chronicle of the United States and Vietnam*, ed. Robert Manning and Michael Janeway, pp. 196–212. Boston: Little, Brown & Co., 1969.

Time, 3 Jan. 1972–6 Nov. 1972.

Toma, Peter A. *The Politics of Food for Peace: Executive-Legislative Interaction*. Institute of Government Research, American Government Series, no. 2. Tucson: University of Arizona Press, 1967.

U.S. Congress. House. Committee on Agriculture. *Review of Public Law 480, the Food for Peace Program.* 104th Congress, 1st sess., 21 June 1995.

———. House. Committee on Foreign Affairs. *Issues Related to the Reauthorization of Food for Peace and Agricultural Export Promotion Programs.* 101st Congress, 2d. sess., 1990.

———. House. Subcommittee on Foreign Agricultural Policy. *Food for Peace, 1954–1978—Major Changes in Legislation.* 96th Cong., 1st sess., 1979.

———. Senate. *Congressional Record.* 88th Cong., 1st sess., 1963. Vol. 109, pp. 96–102.

U.S. Department of Commerce. Bureau of the Census. *Historical Statistics of the United States: Colonial Times to 1970, Part 1, Bicentennial Edition.* Washington D.C.: Government Printing Office, 1975.

Wallerstein, Mitchel B. *Food for War—Food for Peace: United States Food Aid in a Global Context.* Cambridge, Mass.: MIT Press, 1980.

Webb, Daryl. "Crusade: George McGovern's Opposition to the Vietnam War." *South Dakota History* 28 (Fall 1998): 161–90.

Webb, Robert G. "The Pacific Odyssey of Capt. William H. Daly and the 147th Field Artillery Regiment, 1941–1946." *South Dakota History* 23 (Summer 1993): 101–21.

Weber, Max. *The Theory of Social and Economic Organization.* Trans. A. M. Henderson and Talcott Parsons. New York: Oxford University Press, 1947.

Weeks, John R. *Population: An Introduction to Concepts and Issues.* 8th ed. Belmont, Calif.: Wadsworth, 2002.

Weil, Gordon L. *The Long Shot: George McGovern Runs for President.* New York: W. W. Norton & Co., 1973.

White, Theodore H. *The Making of the President, 1972.* New York: Antheneum Publishers, 1973.

World Bank. *World Development Report, 2000/2001: Attacking Poverty.* New York: Oxford University Press, 2001.

"Youthful Volunteers Aid Dozens of 1970 Campaigns," *Congressional Quarterly* 28 (28 Oct. 1970): 2691.

CONTRIBUTORS

GARY AGUIAR is associate professor of political science at South
Dakota State University in Brookings, where he teaches courses
in American politics and public policy. His research interests and
published chapters and articles center on the interplay among
groups in democracy, including questions of group identity and
membership. He is currently working on a book about rural and
small-town politics in America.

AHRAR AHMAD is professor of political science at Black Hills State
University in Spearfish, South Dakota, where he teaches courses on
comparative politics and international relations. He has published
on issues related to the causes of development and underdevelopment in South Asia and is currently engaged in an exploration
of the relationship between Islam and democracy. Ahmad has received many research grants and was selected by the students at
BHSU as the Outstanding Faculty of the Year in 2001/2002.

TOM DASCHLE is the senior United States senator from South Dakota.
In the Senate, he serves as Democratic leader and formerly served
as Senate Majority Leader. Born in Aberdeen, South Dakota,
Daschle was the first person in his family to graduate from college
when he completed his political science degree from South Dakota
State University in 1969. After serving as an intelligence officer
in the United States Air Force and aide to South Dakota senator
James Abourezk, Daschle was elected to the United States House
of Representatives in 1978, where he served until his election to
the Senate in 1986.

THOMAS J. KNOCK is associate professor of history at Southern Methodist University in Texas and served as lecturer in American history at Princeton University. He has authored numerous articles
on American foreign policy, American popular culture, and George
McGovern. His book *To End All Wars: Woodrow Wilson and the
Quest for a New World Order* was awarded the Warren F. Kuehl Prize
by the Society for Historians of American Foreign Relations. Knock
is currently completing the book *Come Home, America: A Political*

Biography of George McGovern. He serves on the editorial board of *Presidential Studies Quarterly* and on the board of the Woodrow Wilson Birthplace and Museum.

LAURIE LANGLAND is university archivist and director of service learning at Dakota Wesleyan University. She has a degree in criminal justice from the University of South Dakota, a law degree from the University of Wisconsin-Madison, and an M.A. in library science from the University of Arizona-Tucson.

VALERIE R. O' REGAN is visiting scholar in the Department of Political Science at California State University, Fullerton. Previously, she served as assistant professor of political science at North Dakota State University. Her publications include the book *Gender Matters: Female Policymakers' Influence in Industrialized Nations* and numerous works concerning gender politics and female gubernatorial candidates.

JON D. SCHAFF is assistant professor of political science at Northern State University in Aberdeen, South Dakota, where he teaches courses on American political institutions and American political thought. His writings on the historical presidency have appeared in *White House Studies, Political Research Quarterly*, and various edited volumes.

DONALD C. SIMMONS, JR., is executive director of the South Dakota Humanities Council and founding director of the South Dakota Center for the Book. Simmons completed his Ph.D. in history and international studies at the University of Denver. He has published over twenty-five scholarly works, including *Confederate Settlements in British Honduras* and *Latin America and the Caribbean in Transition*. He is frequently interviewed by the media and has appeared on C-SPAN's *Book TV* program. In 1997, he received the Presidential Award from the Association of Third World Studies in recognition of his scholarly contributions.

STEPHEN J. STAMBOUGH is assistant professor in the Department of Political Science at California State University, Fullerton. Previously, Stambough served as assistant professor of political science at North Dakota State University. His publications include the book *Initiative-Centered Politics: The New Politics of Direct Democracy* and numerous works concerning electoral politics and female gubernatorial candidates.

MICHAEL J. C. TAYLOR is assistant professor of history at Dickinson State University in North Dakota. Among his publications are biographies of Confederate general P. G. T. Beauregard, Franklin Pierce, and a forthcoming book on Herbert ("Zeppo") Marx. In addition to his research interests in American history and the Civil War, Taylor has studied in Hollywood, recording musical LPs and CDs. He was educated at Cerritos College, Rockhurst College, and the University of Missouri, Kansas City.

STEPHEN K. WARD is academic advisor and coordinator of the Freshman Year Experience Program at the University of South Dakota in Vermillion. He completed his M.A. in history at the University of South Dakota and is a Ph.D. candidate at American University in Washington, D.C. Ward's research interests include McGovern's work in reforming the state and national Democratic parties.

ROBERT P. WATSON is associate professor of political science at Florida Atlantic University and editor of the journal *White House Studies*. He is author or editor of twenty books, including *The Presidents' Wives: Reassessing the Office of First Lady* and *Anticipating Madam President*. He has published over one hundred scholarly articles and essays on the presidency, first ladies, civil rights, environmental policy, and American politics. Watson has been interviewed by CNN, Fox, MSNBC, and *USA Today*, among other media outlets, and has appeared on C-SPAN's *Book TV* program. He directed the first-ever "Report to the First Lady," which was presented to the White House in 2001, and serves on the governing boards of several presidential foundations and scholarly journals.

RUSSELL E. WILLIS is provost and chief academic officer at Champlain College in Burlington, Vermont. He was the former vice-president of academic affairs and dean of the faculty at Dakota Wesleyan University in Mitchell, South Dakota. While at DWU, Willis also served as founding director of the George and Eleanor McGovern Library and Center for Public Service. In 2002, he coordinated the inaugural McGovern Conference at DWU with the theme "Ending Hunger in Our Time." Willis earned his Ph.D. in ethics and society from Emory University and his M.S. in engineering and management and his M.Th. (Theology) from Southern Methodist University in Texas.

INDEX

Stevenson, Adlai, xi, 51, 164
Strategic Hamlet program, 169
Sutton, Percy, 104–5

Tax reductions, 112
Tennyson, Alfred Lord, 155
Terrorism: causes of, 151–52,
176–77
*Terry: My Daughter's Life-and-
Death Struggle with Alcoholism*
(1996), 146
Thailand, 69
*Third Freedom: Ending Hunger in
Our Time* (2001), 152, 176
Thorsness, Leo, 55
Time, 120, 131
A Time of War, a Time of Peace
(1968), 145
Topeka, Kan., 24
Treaty of Versailles: violation of,
20
Truman, Harry S: 20, 74; policy of
containment, 164

Unemployment, 172
United Nations, 20, 77
United Nations Food and Agri-
culture Organization, 156,
160; McGovern appointed U.S.
ambassador to, 146, 174–77
United Nations Food Conference,
86
United Nations Relief and Reha-
bilitation Association, 77
United Nations Resolution 1496,
78
United States Army Air Forces:
McGovern in, 10, 19–30, 160–
63
United States Department of
Agriculture, 72
United States Office of the Foreign
War Relief, 71

United States Relief Committee
for China, 71
United States Senate Committee
on Agriculture, 55, 56, 76, 176
United States Senate Committee
on Foreign Affairs, 56
United States Senate Committee
on the Interior, 56
United States Senate Select Com-
mittee on Nutrition and Human
Needs, 55
United Steelworkers of America,
101, 127
University of Berlin, 143
University of Innsbruck, 143
University of New Orleans, 143
University of Pennsylvania, 143

Valko, Mike, 26, 28–30
Vietnam Antiwar Movement
Conference, 1990, 145
*Vietnam: Four American Perspec-
tives* (1990), 145
Vietnam: McGovern's visit to,
31–34
Vietnam War, 92–97, 112, 167;
McGovern's opposition to, 31–
34, 54, 57–58, 112; in the 1972
presidential election, 129–34
Vis: McGovern lands at, 27–28
*Vital Center: The Politics of Free-
dom, The*, 161
Voting records: of McGovern,
59–65

Wade, Richard C., 100, 109, 112,
115n.24
Wall Street Journal, 155
Wallace, George, 98, 103–4, 120,
121
Wallace, Henry, 14, 72, 164
War: description of, 19–21. *See
also* Vietnam War; World War II

CPSIA information can be obtained
at www.ICGtesting.com
Printed in the USA
FFHW022052070819
54165658-59882FF